THE
GIANT'S CAUSEWAY
AND THE NORTH ANTRIM COAST

Born and raised in Belfast, **Philip Watson** is an ecologist and writer who has carried out contract studies and volunteer work in numerous countries across three continents, on islands and at sea around Ireland and in the North and South Atlantic. Twelve years on the field staff of the National Trust, based at the Giant's Causeway, were followed by early retirement in 1999 to spend more time doing fieldwork and writing. His north coast trilogy comprises this updated Giant's Causeway book, *Rathlin: Nature and Folklore* (2011) and *A Companion to the Causeway Coast Way* (2004). He also broadcasts regularly on natural and local history projects and has written and read stories for radio. A recent project has been the creation of fifty illustrated sea fables for his two grandchildren.

THE
GIANT'S CAUSEWAY
AND THE NORTH ANTRIM COAST

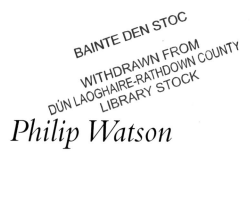
Philip Watson

THE O'BRIEN PRESS
DUBLIN

This revised edition published 2018.

First published 2000 by The O'Brien Press Ltd.,

12 Terenure Road East, Rathgar, Dublin 6, Ireland.

Tel: +353 1 4923333; Fax: +353 1 4922777

E-mail books@obrien.ie

Website www.obrien.ie

Revised and extended 2000, 2012

Originally published in 1992 by HMSO Belfast

and the Environment and Heritage Service,

now the Northern Ireland Environment Agency.

The O'Brien Press is a member of Publishing Ireland.

ISBN: 978-1-84717-996-8

4 6 8 10 9 7 5

18 20 22 24 23 21 19

Layout, editing, typesetting and design: The O'Brien Press Ltd.

Printed and bound by Drukarnia Skleniarz, Poland

The paper in this book is produced using pulp from managed forests

Published in:

DUBLIN

UNESCO
City of Literature

CONTENTS

PREFACE TO THIS EDITION

This book can be traced back twenty six years to my first account of the site in *The Giant's Causeway, "a remnant of chaos …"* published in 1992 by Her Majesty's Stationery Office (HMSO). There followed a more comprehensive book with the present title, published by The O'Brien Press in 2000 and reprinted in 2006. A significant revision and enlargement was published in 2012 to coincide with the opening of the present Visitor Centre. Six years on, some further updates have been included in the text of this 2018 edition.

Like William Thackeray – the Victorian novelist and author of *The Irish Sketchbook of 1842* who took a boat trip to the famous stones in the autumn of that year – I had my first view of the Giant's Causeway and its spectacular coastline from a small boat on a heaving sea. Fisheries studies in the early 1970s took me in and out of the Causeway bays, under magnificent headlands, in pursuit of lobsters and crabs. Earlier work on birds and later ecological and local history surveys involved exploring the north coast and its islands on foot, and I have retained an intimate association with the area for over fifty years.

Having enjoyed the privileges of such close contact with the local fishing and other communities, and the plants and animals of the sea and land, my perception of the Causeway Coast is one of superb landscapes and seascapes, populated and visited by interesting people and supporting a wealth of wildlife.

In these pages, the origins of the strange stones of the Giant's Causeway are part of equally fascinating stories of fishermen, farmers, seaweed-gatherers, smugglers, boatmen, guides, storytellers, artists, poets, writers, philosophers, scientists, naturalists, travellers, tourists and celebrities. Thus it has not been difficult to prove that the famous eighteenth-century author and wit Doctor Samuel Johnson, reluctant to visit Ireland, was wrong when he responded to his biographer James Boswell's question 'Is not the Giant's Causeway worth seeing?' with his now famous answer 'Worth seeing, yes, but not worth going to see.'

Philip S. Watson

INTRODUCTION

WELCOMING THE WORLD

WHERE THE NORTH COAST OF IRELAND FACES THE ATLANTIC OCEAN, WITH SCOTLAND VISIBLE ACROSS THE WATER ON CLEAR DAYS, A HUGE PAVEMENT OF SYMMETRICAL COLUMNS OF A DARK ROCK CALLED BASALT DESCENDS FROM THE BASE OF HIGH CLIFFS INTO THE WATER. DID A GIANT WITH A BUILDING BEE IN HIS BONNET CREATE THIS HONEYCOMB-LIKE CAUSEWAY, OR HAD THIS MYSTERIOUS PLACE A NATURAL ORIGIN?

The Giant's Causeway in the twenty-first century retains its beauty and mystery, but it is a very busy place, anticipating a million visitors a year within the present decade arriving from all over the world to ponder the above question, such is the drawing power of the site. These volcanic rocks are just under 60 million years old and are steeped in myths and legends, but before we wind the clock far back to examine geology and giants, it is useful to start in the present.

The site is easily accessible; it is on the north coast of County Antrim about 100 kilometres (just over sixty miles) north of Belfast, Northern Ireland's capital city. The nearest town, three kilometres (two miles) from the Causeway, is Bushmills – a name known to all who appreciate Irish whiskey.

The Visitor Centre, opened in 2012, is the gateway to the Giant's Causeway. Partly tucked into the hillside, it explains in various formats the area's myths and legends, social history, wildlife and conservation. There is a large-screen show featuring the two choices concerning the Causeway's origins – giants or geology. The shop supplies books, pamphlets, tourist information, various gifts and souvenirs. The cafe offers snacks and a meal menu.

Arriving at the height of summer, one might ask if it is always so busy. It is likely there will be some people about no matter what season one visits. Early in the morning, to watch a summer dawn and a yellow light catch the cliff tops and spill into the deep bays, is a time when there might be few humans about and the cackle of nesting fulmars – a grey and white seabird related to the albatross – carries across from nearby cliffs. Or a winter storm, lashing the Causeway with huge breakers, might be the moment to find solitude. Winter can be dramatic on this exposed north coast. Otherwise, the locals and the visitors share the site and hear accents and languages from various places.

In this book the full Causeway story is told, including the shifting land masses creeping across our watery globe on tectonic plates to create, destroy and recreate continents and oceans; the architects of today's Causeway landscape – fire, water, ice, wind and the relentless weathering away of rocks – remind us of violent events and also the passing of immense, unimaginable periods of time; the colonisation of sea and land by plants, then animals, including the relatively recent arrival of humans; the nearly ten thousand years of our occupation of this north coast; the three hundred or so years since the Causeway's 'discovery' in the late seventeenth century; the myths and legends created to explain these strange stones before the scientists arrived to shine their light of logic; the history of local activities and the rise of tourism; caring for the site today; how technology and diving surveys are revealing new wonders of the sea bed and marine life, and not neglecting some good tales, for storytelling has been a long tradition in this part of the world.

Welcome to Northern Ireland's only (so far) World Heritage Site, a designation bestowed on the Giant's Causeway and its surrounding bays and headlands by the United Nations Education, Scientific and Cultural Organisation (UNESCO) in 1986. The Causeway is a good starting point to explore further west and east along the coast, as the chapter on walking and other tours explains. The recommended reading list at the end of this book will help you to investigate some of the topics and various sites in more depth.

MYTHS AND MISTS
Facts and Fictions

MYTHS PRECEDE SCIENCE AND THE TWO MEET AT THE GIANT'S CAUSEWAY. LONG BEFORE IT BECAME IRELAND'S FIRST WORLD HERITAGE SITE, LOCALS CLAIMED THAT THIS STRANGE ARRANGEMENT OF STONES WAS A WONDER OF THE WORLD; THE IRISH EQUIVALENT OF THE PYRAMIDS, BETTER MADE THAN THE TAJ MAHAL, NOTHING, IT WAS CLAIMED, COULD BE COMPARED TO THE PRECISION AND BEAUTY OF THE CAUSEWAY STONES.

Before it became the Giant's Causeway, the original Irish name for the pillars in the sea was *Clochán na bhFomharaigh*, meaning the 'stepping stones of the Fomorians', a small dark people said to inhabit Ireland in pre-Celtic times, or evil and violent folk of Irish myth – take your pick, the origins are blurred in the mists of time and the uncharted territory where oral tradition met recorded history.

As we shall see later, at the time the Causeway came to the notice of scholars and philosophers of the late seventeenth century, it already had its 'Giant' prefix. How did this happen? Someone special had to be responsible for such a feat of creation, leaving God out of the equation as perhaps His works were on a more global scale. Since early Christian times, tales of Irish heroes known as the Finnian cycle existed. At their heart was Fionn mac Cumhail, an Irish warrior who, around the third century, led a band of elite fighting men known as the Fianna. Fionn the blond combatant (Fionn means 'the fair one'), Fionn the hunter with his favourite hound Bran, Fionn of the knowledge gained from a taste of the magic salmon – such a man was easily mythologised and so it was Fionn, elevated to the status of a giant and anglicised to Finn McCool, that the early Causeway guides, schooled locally in the Finnian tales, turned to find their colossus who made the Giant's Causeway.

It was Finn who tore a great sod of earth from Ulster to hurl at a rival Scottish giant. He missed, as the story goes, and the great lump of a missile landed in the Irish Sea to become the Isle of Man. The hole it left behind flooded to create Lough Neagh, the largest body of freshwater in the British Isles. His name prefixes many villages and towns in Ulster, for example Finvoy, Fintona, Fintown and is even found in Scotland, at Fingal's Cave on the island of Staffa.

Generations of guides at the Causeway embroidered tales of Finn, to the amusement, and occasional irritation, of their customers – a tradition that has not entirely died out. The core of their legend goes something like this:

One of various 'giants' at the Causeway.

A Tale of Two Giants

Long ago, an Irish giant named Finn MacCool roamed the north coast, where he could look across the narrow sea of Moyle to Scotland. A Scottish giant, Benandonner, was Finn's greatest rival, challenging his strength and reputation. As the two giants had never met, Finn decided to invite Benandonner to Ireland, to engage in a decisive battle. There was no boat large enough to carry giants, so Finn built a causeway of huge stones across the water so that the Scottish giant could travel on dry land; thus he would have no excuse to avoid the confrontation.

However, as big Ben approached, Finn realised to his horror that his opponent was a larger and more fearsome rival than he had anticipated. He fled to his home in the nearby hills, and, like any sensible man, asked his wife for advice. Oonagh, a practical woman, disguised Finn as a baby, complete with large nightgown and bonnet. She placed him in a huge, hastily made cradle, telling him to keep quiet and pretend to sleep, as Benandonner's great shadow darkened the door.

Oonagh brought the Scottish giant in for tea, pleading with him not to waken Finn's child.

Looking at the massive 'baby' lying in the cradle, Benandonner took fright, saying that if this was the child, he had no wish to meet the father. He fled back to Scotland, ripping up the Causeway behind him, terrified that the awful Finn might follow him home.

This, claims the legend, is why it is known as the Giant's Causeway. Those who remain sceptical are shown the open water, Scotland on the horizon, and a pile of broken Causeway columns, which mark the destructive haste of the fleeing giant. The Irish may have a reputation for enjoying a fight, but trickery won the battle on this occasion.

Variations on this theme exist, and the story can be extended, with details of the 'child's' exploits. Some tell of Finn building the Causeway to bring home a wife from Scotland, or to visit a lady-love, a giantess. The Scottish giant is sometimes called Fingal, and this name is preserved in Fingal's Cave, the basalt columns on the island of Staffa that locals claim are the other end of Finn MacCool's famous Causeway.

In the above story, he is given the name Benandonner, probably derived from a headland to the east of the Giant's Causeway, known as Benadanir, mentioned later.

To give credence to their tales, the Causeway guides of former years named various physical features in the bays and around the headlands after the giant. Stand on the Causeway and look west, across Port Ganny bay. On the landward side of the Stookans, the little hills at the far end, is the hunched profile of an

Artistic licence at the Organ.

The Giant's Harp – curved columns of basalt.

old woman struggling up the hill. This is the Giant's Granny. She was climbing the hills to supervise Finn as he laboured at building the Causeway; when he could stand her nagging no longer, he turned her to stone. With some help from a modern guide, and a good deal of imagination – perhaps fed by a Bushmills whiskey or two – you might also find in the area the Giant's Harp, the Giant's Eyes, his Organ Pipes, his Chimneys, his Cannons, his Pulpit and more. It may be helpful to refer to the walks recommended in Chapter Seven, with an occasional glance at the maps provided.

The Measure of a Giant

Some will argue that a mythical giant lives best in our minds, and needs no illustration or other evidence. But children (and adults) visiting the Causeway often ask how big Finn MacCool might have been. For the pub-quiz fanatic, the definitive answer is sixteen metres (fifty-two feet and six inches). The clue which leads us to this colossal statistic is the Giant's Boot – a large rock, weathered to the shape of a boot, which lies on the shore in Port Noffer, about 200 metres from the east face of the Causeway. The author – may he be forgiven – took detailed measurements of the Giant's Boot and submitted this evidence, together with photographs, to a number of institutions and scientists. They entered into the spirit of the inquiry, although eventually all but one admitted defeat. The answer came from a forensic anthropologist in South Carolina, who supplied a formula based on her research into ancient footprints. From this came the measure of Finn. So, indeed, myth and science meet at the Giant's Causeway!

Causeway Tales

The stories told by guides over the past three centuries sprang largely from their own imagination and wit, with the giant at their core. There is a rich collection of folklore and stories in the Glens of Antrim, east of the Causeway coast; Cahal Dallat's book *Antrim Coast and Glens: A Personal View* (1990) will give readers a feeling for this. Rathlin Island, lying a few miles off Ballycastle, also has a rich folk history. The folklore of the Causeway is inevitably mixed with traditional beliefs, tales of giants and historical events from the time of the Vikings and earlier.

Some stories are associated with place-names. There is a local belief that Vikings camped, beneath their upturned longboat, at the Brenther harbour in the bay below the Giant's Causeway Centre; the name 'Brenther' is derived from Old Norse words meaning 'steep harbour'.

A more reliable link with Norsemen is found a little way along the coast, at Dunseverick Castle. The Annals of Ulster record that Vikings raided the castle

The Giant's Boot.

twice, in AD870 and AD924; the nearby jagged promontory of Benadanir – 'the peak of the Danes' – is a reminder. Also at Dunseverick, a legend tells how Conal Cearnac, of the Red Branch Knights of Ulster, was present at Christ's crucifixion in Jerusalem, where he subsequently helped push aside the boulder from the mouth of the cave of the resurrection. Another story records how Turlough O'Cahan of Dunseverick returned from the Crusades to find the fortified promontory of his home occupied by the Danes, and his sister forcibly engaged to their leader, Hakon Jarl. Turlough disapproved, and in the ensuing battle both men were killed and the site was burned. The grief-stricken girl leapt to her death from the cliff. Thereafter, it is said, the banshee of the O'Cahans, Granie Roe, could be heard wailing over the roar of the sea in winter storms. (Banshees are female spirits, usually attached to specific families; they are, according to tradition, most noisy around the time of a death.)

The Causeway does not hold a monopoly on giants. The imposing cliffs of Fair Head, near Ballycastle, are 194 metres (636 feet) high, and are composed of huge columns of dolerite, a hard volcanic rock; they are the home of another giant, known as the Grey Man. He has been seen by fishermen in the area, in the shape of a grey-cloaked giant rising from mists swirling over the water and about the headland, in the vicinity of the chasm known as the Grey Man's Path. In 1858 the Grey Man appeared near the Causeway, at the

A daring pose at the Grey Man's Path.

mouth of the River Bush, again, he was a tall, grey-cloaked figure, standing on a pillar of a bridge in a wild flood.

Fairies feature strongly in stories from the Glens of Antrim, but one Causeway tale in particular is worth mentioning. In *Rowlock Rhymes and Songs of Exile* (1933), a book of north Antrim poems in Ulster Scots, there is a tale recorded as 'The Piper and the Fairies'. According to this tale, a local piper by the name of McKibbin was dozing on a Causeway headland after drinking his profits at the end of a Causeway Fair. He was kidnapped by the fairies and taken to a nearby cave, where he remains to this day. McKibbin was also condemned to play the tune 'The Farther in the Deeper' for a hundred years.

For over 300 years, since the Giant's Causeway first became an object of public interest, visitors have been subjected to tall tales as well as to more traditional folk stories. Gradually science crept in, as naturalists, philosophers and geologists debated the natural origin of these unusual rocks. Guides responded to their more serious patrons, who wanted some solid information, and began to slip in a bit of geology – while never letting the facts ruin a good story. Giants, perhaps, earned them larger tips than geology.

The guide performed his office satisfactorily and most obligingly but it would be an improvement if guides could be brought to describe natural appearances correctly and omit the senseless jargon about Giants.

This dry comment was written on 7 April 1876, by the President of the Geological Society of Glasgow, in the logbook of Causeway guide John MacLaughlin. John had netted a serious academic in his daily trawl of customers. Others, in search of entertainment, were more appreciative of his wit and blarney, which were proffered readily, if at a price:

We the undersigned sojourners in this land whose air is fatal to small silver placed ourselves in the hands of our guide the genial John MacLaughlin and found him an honor in his Profession and cheerfully recommend him to all Travelers. Signed, Henry Miller and Chas. H. Edgar of New York and H.A. Potter of Philadelphia, July 1877.

A REMNANT OF CHAOS
Geology and Scientists

M ON DIEU! *AND HAVE I TRAVELLED A HUNDRED AND FIFTY MILES TO SEE* THAT?

The Egg that Cracked

Thackeray chose the ideal phrase when he described the Giant's Causeway as 'a remnant of chaos'. The original chaos was on a much larger scale, and a long time ago.

The crust of the Earth has been likened to a broken eggshell. The giant fragments are called tectonic plates. These are continuously on the move, pulling apart, crashing together or one sliding below the other. In these giant shifts of the Earth's sub-surface continents are formed and pulled apart, mountains are pushed up and oceans come and go. A split in the mass that was the North American and Eurasian plates gradually developed and the North Atlantic Ocean was born and began to widen, between 200 and 100 million years ago. It continues to expand, spreading at a rate of about 20 millimetres per year.

These plate interactions cause earthquakes and volcanic eruptions. The lavas that created the Giant's Causeway were flowing about 60 million years ago, part of an arc of fire

William Thackeray visits the Causeway, 1842.

that took in Greenland, Iceland, Scotland and north-east Ireland. The igneous (Latin *igni* meaning fire) rocks that remain today in these countries have many similarities. Now, the volcanic activity is spread along the North Atlantic ocean ridge, most of it far offshore and deep down in the abyssal zone but active on the surface at Iceland, as disruptive ash clouds drifting south over Europe in 2010 and 2011 aptly demonstrated.

The True Story of the Giant's Causeway

Lava cools and becomes rock. At the Causeway, this is a fine-grained hard rock called basalt. The immediate impression is one of amazing regularity; the whole Causeway looks man-made. The individual columns – remnants of a deep lava-flow – are mainly five- or six-sided; they are so tightly packed that they form a pavement-like structure. The causeways – there are three promontories – extend into the sea but do not, despite the legends, continue underwater to Scotland; the strange stone formations cease quite abruptly, and the seabed offshore is largely composed of sand, shell and gravel (as described in Chapter 7). Large, angular boulders between the causeways are the fractured remains of hard intruded dykes, where later lava flows forced their way to the surface through weaknesses in the ground.

The natural origin of the Giant's Causeway, which was formed just under 60 million years ago, is generally understood to have occurred as follows:

Imagine lava at 1,100°C – eleven times hotter than boiling water – hissing and sparking its way into a hollow, which was probably once a river valley. The lava begins to cool, losing heat to the rocks below and the air above. Cracks zigzag across the surfaces, shattering the shiny new rock to give a honeycomb effect. As the cooling and shrinking progresses through the depth of this volcanic pond, columns are formed. These cool throughout their length, and stresses cause curved cross-cracks, splitting the columns into amazingly equal-sized tablets of stone, each one fitting on the next like a ball-and-socket joint. The result is a geometrical layout of rocks, like a huge, uneven patio. Domes and hollows are obvious features on the top of the Causeway, and the shallow depressions in the tops of the columns nearest the sea are often glittering with salt crystals where little pools of sea water have evaporated.

If the cooling process had been perfectly even, all the columns would have six sides, like the cells of a honeycomb – nature's economy seeking the most efficient way to fill a space. But cooling varied, influenced by seeping fresh water, and amongst the 40,000 or so columns of the Giant's Causeway are some

Former lava flows in cliffs opposite the Causeway.

with four, five, seven, eight or even nine sides. You may be lucky and find the only three-sided stone.

What makes the Causeway special is the fact that it offers a chance to see this wonderful jointing, in both the vertical and the horizontal forms, so easily. This is rare: it is more usual to find columns of basalt partly exposed in cliff-faces – as can be seen within the World Heritage Site at locations such as the Organ, the Amphitheatre and especially Plaiskin Head, all of which are visible from the Causeway and Dunseverick Castle walks described in Chapter 8 (see maps). A spectacular display of columns in a cliff and cave exists at Fingal's Cave on the Scottish island of Staffa, which lies off Mull, a little over 100 kilometres (sixty miles) over the sea to the north of the Causeway.

Visitors often ask if the Causeway was made by hot lava cooling suddenly in the sea, or if it grew like crystals. Although crystals do occur in parts of the Causeway coast lava flows, in hollows created by former gas bubbles, the Causeway columns are not themselves crystals. Neither are they the product of lava sizzling and spluttering into the sea. Between 60 and 55 million years ago, when the Causeway lava was flowing, the sea level was much lower, thus the lava cooled in the air, or on existing cool rocks. If it had poured into the sea, features such as pillow lavas would be found. Where fresh water invaded or flooded the cooling lavas, much more uneven surfaces formed, as can be seen immediately above the Organ and elsewhere along the cliffs.

Local people are very proud of the Giant's Causeway; early guides were inclined to boast that no such thing existed anywhere else in the world. Scientists, unfortunately, often explode myths, and they have discovered columns of basalt similar to the Causeway in many countries. Few, however, are as much visited, wondered at and mythologised as these stepping stones curving gently towards Scotland from Ireland's Atlantic north coast.

The volcanic features are not restricted to the Causeway itself. Three major layers of basalt make up a sandwich-cake of geology along the Causeway coast cliffs, with the icing between the layers represented by red and brown laterite (from the Latin *later*, a brick), which contains iron and bauxite ores. Further east, near Port Moon, and inland, these ores were mined to produce iron and aluminium, the peak extractions being in the 1870s.

Opposite the Giant's Causeway, looking east towards the isolated pillars known as the Chimneys, up to seven lava flows can be identified. The lower basalts are distinct here: about five dark bands in the cliffs, from sea level up to a broad streak of red laterite. This colourful layer separates the lower basalts from the middle basalts, which contain the spectacular columns and similar structures, such as the nearby distinctive arrangement of pillars known as the Organ. Further inland, there is another deep band of reddish inter-basaltic soils, on top of which sit the upper basalts, which are non-columnar. Along the coast further to the west, these stretch down to sea level; but erosion over a long period has removed them from the Causeway area.

'The Chimneys' at Port na Spaniagh.

This arch collapsed in the 1940s.

The many layers of lava flows – some with perfect columns, some with starchy, twisted, cruder columns, some of irregular shape – together with the red, brown, purple and grey inter-basaltic bands, can be viewed along the cliff-top path from major headlands such as Plaiskin, Benbane and Bengore. The bays, headlands and promontories from Portnaboe to Benbane Head show classic features of the geology of the Tertiary period, which lasted from about 65 million to around 2 million years ago. This was one of several volcanic times in the Earth's history, and the superb legacies of the Tertiary, which have survived in the Causeway landscape, are rightly recognised by the World Heritage Convention.

The coastline we see today has been shaped by millions of years of weathering under near-tropical conditions; by ice ages, the most recent of which ended between 20,000 and 10,000 years ago; and by the attacks of the sea when, due to melted ice sheets, the ocean level was much higher than it is today. The relentless wear and tear of rain and wind and frost also helped to sculpt the coast and continues to affect its rocks and soils. All these conditions produced the stepped landscapes, great curved bays, leaving narrow necks and headlands where the sea still takes bites out of the land. In addition to volcanic features such as extruded lava flows and intruded dykes, the coastline includes raised boulder beaches, rock platforms, islets and sea stacks – some of the latter the remains of collapsed arches. All these provide clues to landscape formation, and are reminders that this remains a dynamic coastline.

Even if you are not interested in geology, you cannot fail to be impressed by the colours and the rugged beauty of the Causeway's surroundings.

FROM BISHOPS TO BIOLOGISTS
Discovery and Descriptions

3

IN 1692, WILLIAM KING, THE ANGLICAN BISHOP OF DERRY, AND AN UNNAMED CAMBRIDGE GRADUATE VISITED THE GIANT'S CAUSEWAY. TRAVEL IN IRELAND WAS DIFFICULT IN THOSE DAYS, AND ACCOMMODATION WAS SCARCE AND OFTEN OF POOR QUALITY. THE BISHOP AND HIS COMPANION WERE CREDITED WITH THE 'DISCOVERY' OF THE GIANT'S CAUSEWAY. HOWEVER, A FEW YEARS EARLIER, THE SITE HAD ALREADY COME TO THE ATTENTION OF MEMBERS OF THE ROYAL SOCIETY IN LONDON.

Discoveries of phenomena such as the Giant's Causeway have often been credited to the person or persons who first publicised their finds. Given the site's old Irish name, as mentioned in the previous chapter, it was very likely that it was known to local people for a considerable period prior to the attentions of philosophers and naturalists in the late-seventeenth century. Much the same could be said for the columnar basalts of Fingal's Cave on the Scottish island of Staffa to the north of County Antrim – in 1772 these were shown by locals to the great travelling naturalist Sir Joseph Banks who brought them to wider attention.

At the Royal Society's meeting on 23 January 1689, two letters by Sir Robert Redding were presented. One included a description of *ye Giants Causey* (sic) near Dunluce Castle, mentioning the many hexagonal pillars of stone and this was duly recorded in the Society's minutes and copy book. A later description by Sir Richard Bulkeley of County Wicklow in Ireland, who had obtained details from the above Cambridge scholar, appeared in the *Philosophical Transactions of the Royal Society* in 1693, and this, as far as is known, is the first published account of the Giant's Causeway. Redding had travelled in the north of Ireland in 1688 and it is possible, given his interest in rocks and minerals, that he visited the site, but this remains unconfirmed. Redding died in 1689, and it was left to others to 'elucidate the whole', as later guides were inclined to say when expounding on the wonders of the Causeway.

Between 1692 and 1708, a number of eminent clerics, scholars and natural philosophers commented on the newly discovered Giant's Causeway. Dr Samuel Foley, Bishop of Down and Connor, who contributed his views on the Causeway to the Royal Society in 1694, also included the first known image, an engraving by Christopher Cole, although the site did not appear on a map until 1714. Sir Thomas Molyneux, to become in 1717 Professor of Medicine at Trinity College in Dublin, was interested in geology, archaeology and history and wrote a detailed description of the Causeway and arranged for a sketch of the site to be made by Edward Sandys in 1696. Molyneux was, in this case, something of a proxy fieldworker, for he never visited the Giant's Causeway, basing his accounts on the work of others, including drawings. Although previous literature on the site's early visitors records that Sir Thomas did travel there, recent research (Kennedy, 2008) has shown that it was his nephew Samuel Molyneux who braved the trip as described in his *Journey to ye North, August 7th, 1708*. Samuel encountered the lack of comfort of the day, describing his accommodation at one town near the Causeway as a 'drunken, Stinking Kennel'. Sir Thomas wrote scathingly of the stories of giants, claiming that those with no knowledge of natural history were usually inclined, when faced with natural phenomena they could not understand, to name them after giants, fairies, devils, demons and suchlike. Various rock structures around the world, many columnar, are indeed so named, for examples the Devil's Postpile in California, the Devil's Tower in Wyoming, Fingal's Cave in Scotland (Fingal being a Scottish version of Finn McCool), the Giant's Causeway in New South Wales (also known as Pooningbah, an aboriginal site where the rock columns were believed to be the spines of a giant echidna, a spiny porcupine-like creature native to Australia) and the Adamantine Gates of Hell in Tasmania.

Following this initial flurry of interest in the early 1700s, the next visitor to bring fame to the Giant's Causeway was of a very different nature to the philosophising naturalists. This was a previously unknown Dublin artist, Susanna Drury, who entered a competition to encourage the arts and travelled to the site to create several detailed paintings in 1739 (Anglesea and Preston, 1980), winning a prize in 1740 from the Dublin Society of twenty-five pounds for her work We have to admire the determination of this middle-class artist in making the journey from Dublin to paint, over a stay of three months during which she

A view of the headlands from Hamilton's Seat.

visited the Causeway almost every day, the first landscapes of the site, and the most accurate (allowing for some romantic interpretations) images of the time. Detailed engravings of Drury's paintings were produced by François Vivarès in 1743–44, and the circulation of these around Europe revived interest in the Giant's Causeway, enabling scientists and others to form various theories about the formation of such rocks.

Neptune versus Vulcan

This heavyweight contest in the late 1700s was conducted for the sake of knowledge and of scientific honours. Scientists are as capable of passionate argument as any other human beings. Throughout the eighteenth century, the science of geology was undergoing upheavals, as debates on the origins of the Earth's rocks heated up. Igneous rocks, such as granites and basalts, featured in these controversies, which ran almost as hot as the Causeway lava.

Scientists studying the origins of basalts and similar rocks fell into two camps. Those supporting the theory of fiery origins were labelled Vulcanists, while those who believed in marine sediments as the source were known as Neptunists. Thanks to the Drury/Vivarès illustrations, the Giant's Causeway was known to these learned men.

In the Vulcanists' corner, the main contenders were Nicholas Desmarest of France (1725-1815) and James Hutton (1726-1797), a famous Scottish geologist. Leading the Neptunist contingent were Abraham Werner (1749-1817), a charismatic and influential German teacher of geology, and one R. Kirwan from Ireland, who, in the 1790s, brought the debate to the local scene on the Causeway coast: he claimed to have discovered marine fossils in basalt at Portrush in Co Antrim, near the Giant's Causeway. These fossils are embedded in layers of an ancient shale, 150 million years older than the lava which baked these sediments hard. Kirwan's case, published in 1799, was soon disproved. By the 1820s, the theories of the Vulcanists were generally accepted, and the origin of the Giant's Causeway was no longer seriously disputed.

The Portrush rock (not the sweet type with letters all the way through!) is now a National Nature Reserve, and is well worth a visit. It is on the shore by Ramore Head car park, facing Portrush's East Strand. The nearby Portrush Countryside Centre provides a wealth of information on the natural and local history of the Causeway coast, including these famous debates.

Absent from these arguments were the views of another local man, the Reverend Doctor William Hamilton, a keen naturalist and rector of a nearby Co Donegal parish, who spent the summer of 1784 exploring the Causeway headlands, sometimes on horseback. Hamilton's letters on the natural history of basalt were first published in 1786. He correctly interpreted the Causeway and its surroundings as volcanic in origin, and his writings were the first to relate the Causeway to accurate descriptions of the surrounding landscape. Hamilton's Seat, opposite Plaiskin Head, which was one of the Reverend Doctor's favourite spots, is named in his memory. Sadly, he was murdered near Lough Swilly in Donegal in 1797, in the unrest preceding the rebellion of 1798.

Geologists continued to take a great interest in this coastline, and the mid-twentieth century saw significant developments in the study of basalts. In 1940, the Russian-born geologist Sergei Ivanovich Tomkieff developed a new way of describing the main features of the Causeway. In an interesting alternative view to the Romantic movement's earlier fascination with nature as architecture, he saw in the levels of columnar basalt flows a parallel with classical Greek temple architecture. The lower, regular columns of a typical Causeway flow he called the *colonnade*; the less regular layer above he dubbed the *entablature*. This is exemplified in the Organ, where the tall columns resemble the colonnade (or pillars) of a temple, supporting the entablature (the blocks laid across the top) – in this case, the tightly packed, rather prismatic rock above the Organ.

The Romantics

The Reverend Hamilton referred to the Causeway coast scenery as 'natural architecture'. He lived at the beginning of the Romantic movement, which saw links between art and nature. In the Georgian periods, visitors to the Causeway were seeking a renewal of the human spirit and a chance to immerse themselves in romantic landscapes. Such places were described in language that depicted columns, cliffs and caves as Gothic cathedrals and palaces. Engravings from this period exaggerated the cliff scenery of the area and took artistic licence with the number and size of the Causeway columns. This led to some visitors being disappointed with the reality, as we shall see later.

Poets, too, were attracted by this romantic view of nature and visited the Causeway at this time. Sir Walter Scott, arriving in 1814, was feeling unwell and not inclined to lavish descriptions – unlike W.H. Drummond, who, in the following extract from his epic 1811 Causeway poem, appears to have a partial understanding of the Vulcanists' views:

> Did plastic nature in the flood of flame
> Each hexagon, concave and convex frame?
> Then, did refrigeration's gelid power
> Freeze the dense column, pyramid and tower?

Appreciation of the sublime seems to have been high on visitors' agendas throughout this period, when nature, art and the human response to both of these were in vogue. Edmund Burke, who in 1757 wrote of the sublime as 'a sort of tranquility tinged with terror', saw in the oceans' various moods an expression of this human need for a response to wildness in nature. The Causeway landscape obviously fulfilled this need. In 1845, one Richard Lowry from the north of England, taking a boat trip at the Causeway, recorded in his diary:

… floating upon the bosom of the mighty Atlantic – the sight was certainly grand … At no other spot can the sublime scenery be seen with so much effect.

Guidebooks and Travel Writers

In 1788 one of the first popular guidebooks, entitled *The Complete Irish Traveller in the Kingdom of Ireland*, was published in two volumes. This contained a good description of the Giant's Causeway.

The Belfast Naturalists' Field Club at the Causeway, 11 June 1868.

Fossils of ammonites in Lias shale at Portrush.

Guidebooks proliferated during the 1830s and 1840s, by which time almost all travellers in Ireland had the Causeway on their itinerary. Regular features about the famous stones appeared in popular magazines of the nineteenth century, such as the *Dublin Penny Journal* and the *Illustrated London News*.

Naturalists, many travelling in field club excursions, were anxious to see the Giant's Causeway and air their new-found knowledge, gleaned from the rising tide of geological papers that included references to the Causeway. Photography, too, was contributing to interest in the site; prints were published in the 1860s, and by the 1880s and 1890s these photographs were appearing regularly in guidebooks, alongside the more traditional engravings and sketches.

People and Nature

The rugged terrain around the Causeway has little evidence of early human settlement. In the grasslands and scrub set back a short distance from the coast, however, archaeologists have identified some burial sites, former settlements, hiding places, ritual sites and standing stones, spanning almost 7,000 years, from around 5,000BC (the transition from the Middle to the New Stone Age) to the arrival of the Anglo-Normans in the twelfth century. For example, there are Stone Age tombs, which required some degree of co-operation to build, along the ridges just inland of Ballintoy. There are many other ancient sites in the area, dating from periods ranging from the Bronze Age (around 2,500BC) to the time of the Vikings' arrival (the ninth and tenth centuries AD). For example, there are two fine double-ringed earthworks at Lisanduff, above Portballintrae car park; and a number of circular earthworks or raths are scattered along the coastal hinterland. Souterrains (man-made underground passages lined with stone, used for storage and as hiding places) are also found in the area – at Aird, near the Causeway, for example, and at Dunluce Castle. Add to these the

The shale and lava beds at Portrush, which featured in eighteenth-century geological debates.

occasional standing stones, promontory forts (for example, at Larrybane, near Carrick-a-Rede) and a few caches of buried Viking ornaments and coins, and the north coast has its fair share of what local archaeologist Jon Marshall has referred to as 'forgotten places'.

The philosophers, romantics and geologists who took an early interest in the Giant's Causeway gave way to a rising tide of tourism, and it was quite a long time before the biologists arrived to list and study the varieties of plants and animals that had established themselves and adapted to local conditions following the last ice age. Their work and findings are considered in Chapter 6.

MAKING A LIVING
Local Life and Natural Resources

PEOPLE HAVE BEEN COMING TO THE CAUSEWAY COAST FOR A LONG TIME. EXCAVATIONS AT A MESOLITHIC SITE AT MOUNT SANDEL ON THE RIVER BANN, JUST UPSTREAM FROM COLERAINE, SHOWED THAT A SETTLEMENT EXISTED THERE ABOUT 9,000 YEARS AGO. IN ADDITION TO GATHERING FOOD FROM THE NEARBY WOODLANDS AND FROM THE RIVER, THE INHABITANTS MADE EXPEDITIONS TO THE COAST TO CATCH FISH IN THE RIVER ESTUARY AND PERHAPS TO GATHER SHELLFISH ALONG THE SHORELINE. ABOUT 5,000 YEARS AGO, NEOLITHIC DUNE-DWELLERS AROUND THE COAST ALSO GATHERED SHELLFISH AND CAUGHT BIRDS. THE RELIANCE ON COLONIES OF SEABIRDS AND THEIR EGGS AS SOURCES OF FOOD WAS COMMON TO ISLAND COMMUNITIES OFF NORTHWEST SCOTLAND AND AROUND THE IRISH COAST, FROM RATHLIN AT THE EASTERN END OF THE CAUSEWAY COAST TO THE BLASKETS OFF CO KERRY. THESE ACTIVITIES ONLY CEASED WITHIN LIVING MEMORY; AS RECENTLY AS THE 1940s, GULLS' EGGS WERE HARVESTED AT RATHLIN.

There were risks in exploiting the natural resources of the sea, whether by venturing out in small boats to fish, by collecting seabirds and their eggs from cliffs and rock stacks, or by gathering seaweed at the foot of towering headlands. Even those in larger ships were not always safe, as lists of known shipwrecks around this north coast testify.

Fisheries

Along this rugged coast, men have rowed, sailed and chugged to sea in small boats for over 350 years in pursuit of fish. The 1825 *Steamboat Companion to the Western Islands and Highlands of Scotland* reported that fishing boats from Portnahaven on the island of Islay were travelling the thirty miles to the Giant's Causeway to fish for cod, ling and turbot. As recently as 1926, the small harbours nearest to the Causeway – Portballintrae and Dunseverick – sheltered twenty working boats supporting fifty-four fishermen, including those who worked part-time. Due to declines in fish stocks, increased freight charges and alternative employment ashore, there are few full-time fishermen making a living today.

As well as fixing salmon nets at various shore stations, fishermen caught lobster, edible crab, buckies (whelks), cod, haddock, skate, ling, plaice and other fish living on or near the seabed. Fish nearer the surface, such as herring and mackerel, were also taken. In the 1920s and 30s, fishermen set long lines – some a mile in length – using hooks baited with mussels, limpets, salted mackerel or buckies. This method exploited fish stocks throughout the year, with hard days at sea in pursuit of winter cod.

The north Antrim fishermen worked in traditional boats, long lining for fish and potting for crab, lobster and buckies. Some had the advantage of an inboard engine for powering the boat, but others rowed or sailed. Without navigational instruments, the fishermen relied on long-established sight-lines to landmarks ashore to locate fishing grounds. Out of Dunseverick, for example, if a fisherman lined up the Carrick-a-Rede bridge with the north side of Sheep Island, the Causeway Stookans past the Chimneys and the Dunseverick Stookan, he would have been on a good ridge for cod. The fishermen's knowledge of the sea, and of the creatures they sought, was remarkable.

The sketch of Thackeray at sea off the Causeway in 1842, in his *Irish Sketch Book*, is notable in that it records very accurately the traditional boat of the north Irish coast at this time – a double-ended *drontheim*, otherwise known as a Norway yawl. These seaworthy vessels survived as fishing-boats well into the twentieth century, and they were a common sight in small coves and harbours around the Donegal and Antrim coasts, as well as on the Scottish island of Islay. There is a revival of interest in *drontheims* at present, and the risk that this unique vessel will become extinct has lessened.

The pursuit of salmon around the Irish coast has a long history. Bag nets,

Left: Finn MacCool features in ancient Irish tales as a Celtic warrior, but generations of storytellers at the Causeway saw him as larger than life.

Previous page: The soft light at sunset reddens the details of the Causeway's columns. The cross-fracturing of individual columns – split apart as they cooled from lava to rock – was curved, giving rise to convex and concave surfaces.

Below: The fort of Sobhairce occupied a strategic cliff-top promontory, reputedly once the capital of the Kingdom of Dalriada, where today the gaunt remains of an Elizabethan tower and walls survive, battered by Atlantic winds.

Above: Benandir ('the Peak of the Danes'), a jagged basalt promontory at Port Moon, close to Dunseverick Castle. Vikings raided this area in the ninth and tenth centuries. On this central part of the Causeway Coast, the cliffs gradually drop from a height of over 100 metres (300 feet) to sea level.

Below: From deep in the earth's crust, hot magma – at over 1,000 °C – fed the lava flows. When these cooled, they formed the basalt bones of much of the Causeway Coast's landscape.

Above: There are roughly 40,000 columns, closely packed, in the Giant's Causeway. Guides often told visitors there were 39,996; when asked how they could be so precise, they would say that there had been 40,000, but a rich visitor had bought four and taken them away!

Below: Although most Causeway stones have six sides, there are four-, five-, seven- and even eight-sided exceptions.

Above: *Many lava flows created the layered landscape around the Causeway cliffs. The splashes of rusty red soils give a clue to their origin; long-ago weathering processes formed ores of iron and aluminium.*

Below: *Deep, shady bays and sharp headlands are characteristic of the Causeway World Heritage Site.*

Above: *Susanna Drury's mid-eighteenth-century paintings may have exaggerated the Causeway columns somewhat; nevertheless, they were the first reasonably accurate images, and they created great excitement among geologists of the time.*

Right: *Local guides of the eighteenth and nineteenth centuries gave names to many features — including the pipe-like columns of the Organ — to enhance their stories of the giant who, they claimed, had created the Causeway and the surrounding landscape.*

Above: Yellow skirt sea slug, Okenis elegans.   *Below:* Kelp 'forest' and red seaweeds.

Fishermen in earlier days near the Giant's Causeway.

which took over from fixed draft nets in the 1830s to 1850s, have gradually been phased out as part of salmon conservation schemes, or closed down due to lack of fish. Only two such nets survive at present, at Torr Head and Cushendun.

Fishing has always been a hazardous way of life. Only great knowledge of the sea, and a healthy respect for it, minimised the risks. When the crews of the *drontheims* were working the salmon nets and fishing crabs, the fishermen often transferred their catches to passing fishing-smacks bound for Liverpool. These larger vessels were in such a hurry to return to port with their valuable cargoes that the transfers were made while the smacks were under sail. This sometimes led to tragedies, and crew members were lost when the smaller boats capsized.

Despite the hardships of the deep, humour was never far from surfacing. Consider the Dunseverick advice on seasickness: 'Take a large spoonful of jam before you go to sea – it won't cure the seasickness, but sure it tastes as good coming up as it did going down!'

The Cliff-Climbers

Today, over 170,000 seabirds inhabit the cliffs, rock stacks, coves, caves and surging waters of Rathlin Island. Over a hundred years ago, Victorian naturalists viewed these busy breeding colonies with awe, referring to the 'whirring multitudes' of birds. The islanders had a more pragmatic approach: the birds, and their eggs, provided food over the short nesting season from May to August, and were also preserved for winter sustenance.

Climbing unaided up sea stacks, descending a cliff on a hemp rope or nosing a small boat into a narrow cave and landing on a ledge, the bird-men ducked

Cliff-climbing bird-hunters of Rathlin Island, with ropes, an egg-box, a gun and two freshly killed guillemots.

the roar of wings as panicking birds whizzed past, and took a harvest of eggs and birds to supplement their larders. Despite their remarkable climbing skills and detailed local knowledge, accidents happened; and inevitably, on such huge cliffs, there were fatalities. But in those days, fish and seabirds were important sources of protein, and cash crops were few.

One of these – also provided by the sea – was the annual kelp harvest.

The Story of Kelp

The cold, clear waters of the Atlantic Ocean and North Channel, and their rocky and cliff-bound shores, are ideal for the growth of the large brown seaweeds collectively known as kelp. In spring and summer, thick-stemmed oarweeds and other brown algae grow vigorously in these coastal waters; their wet brown stems and fronds can be seen glinting on the surface at low tide, or waving underwater – like a forest of trees in a gale – as the high tide swirls and pushes around them.

In winter, this rich growth dies off and storms loosen the kelp's hold on the rocks. Large numbers of stems and tangles of weed are washed ashore in coves, bays and beaches along the Causeway coast. In May, the 'cuckoo storms' throw up the last piles of this marine detritus, which is known locally as the 'May fleece'.

Today, these banks of seaweed are left to rot, picked over by birds in search of insects, shellfish and other marine creatures caught up in the tangles. However, from at least the eighteenth century to the 1930s, kelp was an important resource for northern and western coastal communities of Scotland and Ireland.

In the Causeway bays, the seaweed was gathered by hand, and the heavy, wet loads were carried in wicker creels, or on long-handled forks, to be piled to dry on low dry-stone walls specially constructed close to the tide-mark. Remains of kelp walls can be seen in Portnaboe and other bays to the east as far as Ballintoy. When the weed had dried, usually by June or July, it was laid on iron bars or similar grids over stone-lined pits, or kelp kilns, and burned. The molten residue, like a bluish sticky toffee, eventually cooled and hardened, and this product was also called kelp. It was bagged and, in the remoter bays, carried to the cliff-top to be collected by agents.

In a letter dated 13 August 1784, the Reverend Doctor William Hamilton records the fate of one particular kelp-gatherer called Adam Morning, who lived close to the Causeway.

One morning [in the summer of 1783] *as Adam and his wife were descending down the dangerous path to pursue their daily toil, while they were yet talking of their growing hopes, even while the cheerful prospect was smiling in their view, a sudden slip tumbled him headlong from the precipice and dashed him to pieces on the rocks below.*

Despite the risks of the work, kelp-gathering provided an important source of income to the farming and fishing families of the Causeway coast, and on Rathlin it paid the islanders' rents. The salts of sodium and potassium which came from kelp were essential in bleaching processes and in making soap and glass. The later discovery that iodine was present in kelp proved useful in medicine and photography, two applications which prolonged the industry through the late nineteenth century.

By the 1930s, modern methods of recovering large amounts of these chemicals from other sources destroyed the demand for kelp, and even the more recent exploitation of seaweeds for the alginate industry has not revived interest in the commercial value of the Causeway coast's marine algae.

The whitish smoke of kelp fires is no longer seen, but once it was a regular feature in summer on these northern shores. While it was probably an irritant to the kelp-burners, the pungent smoke was believed by some to have

decongestant qualities. There are records that sufferers were prepared to take a lungful or two to alleviate bronchial troubles – perhaps the only case where smoking might have been good for your health!

Scavengers and Smugglers

Beachcombing, especially in the event of shipwrecks, has long been an established activity along the rugged Causeway coast. Many ships have come to grief along this north coast.

In 1588, the wreck of the Spanish Armada ship *Girona* provided James McDonnell of Dunluce Castle with the opportunity to scavenge cannons and treasure, the latter probably in the form of coins and jewels from the bodies washed ashore. Travel writer Edwin Waugh was staying at the Causeway Hotel, which overlooks Blackrock and Bushfoot Strand, when the liner *Cambria* was wrecked in autumn 1870 at the rocky islands of Inishtrahull, off the northern tip of the Inishowen peninsula opposite. Waugh noticed the wreck-gatherers; in his book *Rambles and Revelries*, published in 1874, he wrote:

... as I went towards the strand, I met cart after cart returning from the sea, laden with wreck.

Above: The George A. Hopley, *an American square-rigger, wrecked off Portstewart in 1856.*

Left:
The white smoke of kelp fires is a thing of the past.

Over the years, timber, liquor, cloth, china and many other commodities found their way into local households. During the two World Wars, convoys attacked by submarines added to the list of tragedies, and often poignant personal effects of the sailors' would be washed up on these beaches.

The coastguards at Portballintrae – here pictured just over 100 years ago – were armed and kept busy in pursuit of smugglers. Edwin Waugh, mentioned above, enjoyed a chat with these men in their 'breezy man-o'-war garb', and was shown 'the arms of the station all sharp and bright and ready for

A coastguard at Portballintrae, 1898.

action'. The coastguards' vigilance was particularly sharp in the narrow North Channel, which separates the Co Antrim coast from the Mull of Kintyre by as little as eleven miles. The Campbeltown Customs Records for the years 1739-1816 show that variations in excise duties and other taxes led to smuggling of horses, wool, salt, soap, hides, tea, tobacco and whiskies, both Scotch and Irish.

Jimmy Irvine, writing about the above records in 1976, described the scene:

... the coastlines on North and East Antrim and Kintyre seemed to have been specially designed by nature to assist the smuggler ... the crossing could be made in two or three hours in small open or half decked boats. These would pull up to load and land their secret cargoes in the many lonely creeks and coves with which these shores abound.

In 1812, barley was smuggled from Portballintrae to Islay for the manufacture of whiskey. By 1815, illegal whiskey distillation at Inishowen (north Donegal) had been stopped, and Islay whisky was fetching double the price per gallon when smuggled the thirty miles to the north Antrim coast.

Mr Cross, the coastguard, Portballintrae, 1898.

Fairs and Regattas

Coast and country folk made their own entertainment, combining business with pleasure – as at a country fair where trade was shared with sports – or just getting together to pit their special skills against one another, as at regattas and horse races.

Many country fairs have disappeared over the past 150 years, but some survive. The Lammas Fair of Ballycastle, usually held over two days in the last week of August (although the traditional day of the Irish summer festival of Lammas is the first of August), dates from at least 1606. There was a Causeway Fair in the nineteenth century, and it was revived for a while in later years; it was held in summer in fields by the Causeway Head, with sports and entertainments such as tug-o'-war and pipers. Not all such diversions were in summer. The Bushmills Annual Horse Races were held in January each year on Bushfoot Strand; the first of these Races, in 1877, attracted around 10,000 spectators from townlands around the neighbouring parishes.

With the availability of the skills and strength of men making a living from the sea, it is not surprising to find that sailing and rowing regattas were also popular annual events. Summer regattas were held at most of the north- and east-coast ports, from Moville in

Yellow Man – a sticky toffee – for sale at the Old Lammas Fair in Ballycastle.

Donegal to Carnlough in Antrim. Traditional boats, such as *drontheims* and specially built rowing skiffs for crews of two or four oarsmen, were raced. One famous skiff, the *Arrow* of Port Moon, was celebrated by local poets; their verses, backed up by newspaper reports of the time, provide a record of the vessel's successes. James McAllister of Tonduff, near the Causeway, born in 1865, was probably referring to a regatta in the 1880s when he wrote:

> *The course being selected lay near Ramore Hill*
> *Where the boys from Port Moon met the men from Moville*
> *In their fast racing drontheim called Arrow by name*
> *Her crew and her coxswain – five heroes of fame ...*

The Moville men had a priest along, to bless them as 'kings of the waves', but the crew of the *Arrow* beat them nevertheless! In 1985, the *Arrow* was rescued from decay in the Port Moon fishery bothy, restored and put on display in the Causeway Centre for a number of years. This unique vessel is kept at the National Trust's Education Centre at Innisfree Farm, just up the road from the Visitor Centre.

Causeway-like columns at an inland quarry near Ballintoy.

Mining and Quarrying

Not all commercial activities were sea- and shore-based. Iron and aluminium ores, present in the red soils between lava flows, were mined where these beds were thickest. The mines were spread around the Antrim basalt plateau, from north of Belfast through the Glens of Antrim to the north coast. The peak extractions took place from 1870 to 1880, although some mines continued to operate until the 1920s, and there were examples of old aluminium ore mines being re-opened during the Second World War.

A description of iron mining in Co Antrim was recorded by J. Hodges in his 1875 Presidential Address to the Belfast Natural History and Philosophical Society. He referred to the availability of local labour:

… a very short time was sufficient to convert the ordinary farm labourers of the district into excellent miners, able to pick from two to three tons of ore daily.

At this time, a miner with a little experience earned 15 to 20 shillings weekly.

There was a strong link between mining and quarrying and the development of railways, and tracks for mineral extraction were laid inland to formerly secluded glens, to facilitate transport of ores to shipping ports. The famous Giant's Causeway tram (described later) was conceived as a mineral railway, although it turned out to be a vital link for tourists between the main Portrush–Belfast railway line and the Giant's Causeway.

There were iron and bauxite (aluminium ore) mines along the Causeway coast. Most were driven horizontally into the red bed between the lower and middle basalts, a little way inland; but one was at the coast in Port Fad, just north of Port Moon, on the Causeway headlands. The ore at this site was run on buggies down a small track to a flat point halfway down to the sea, where it was tipped down a chute to small coasters waiting at a rather perilous berth below. It probably joined the ores from east Antrim mines, which were shipped to processing plants in Britain.

The coastal landscape is pitted here and there with the scars of basalt and chalk quarries, but few are active now. Columns of basalt were cut from exposures near Portrush and Ballintoy, and even the Giant's Causeway was not immune to such exploitation, as we shall see later. Many walls, farm outhouses and gate pillars along this coast, if examined closely, show the distinctive Causeway-type stones, which also served the builders of the ancient church of Templastragh, above Port Braddan.

Farming

Before the Second World War, farming in this coastal area coexisted with fishing, kelp-making, mining and quarrying. All these other activities have either died out or declined, and, as subsidies became available, farming intensified in the post-war years.

Much bogland and heath along the north Antrim coast has been converted to pasture, and considerable areas of rough grazing have been improved by the addition of fertilisers to boost grass growth and increase stocking rates of sheep and cattle. Coastal heaths and maritime grasslands, once rich in wild flowers and small birds, have been fragmented, and only patches survive near the cliff edges.

Despite criticism from some that farming has changed the landscape and reduced the diversity of wildlife, many farmers claim to be the custodians of the countryside. For much of this Causeway Coast landscape, they are, and many have opted to join various Environmental Farming Schemes (EFS) offered by the Department of Agriculture, Environment and Rural Affairs (DAERA). These provide advice and funding to improve habitats and encourage native wildlife. Farmers have choices from a wide range of options, such as hedge and dry stone wall creation and maintenance and the provision of seed plants and winter stubble for small birds. The Northern Ireland Environment Agency, part of DAERA, provides additional agri-environment programmes, some more targeted at specific conservation needs, for example helping ground-nesting birds such as lapwing and curlew.

Diversification has led to some other farm-based activities, such as providing bed and breakfast, fishing ponds, pony trekking and even the occasional small golf course. Farming continues to be a dominant influence on this coastal landscape, providing a patchwork of small fields and clustered settlements or *clacháns*, some of which are attracting the attention of developers of holiday homes.

BOATMEN, GUIDES AND ENTERTAINERS
Hosts and Tourists

THIS CHAPTER BEGINS IN THE 1790s, IN THE FINAL PHASE OF THE MORE RELAXED ROMANTIC MOVEMENT'S INTEREST IN THE CAUSEWAY, MOVES ON TO THE 1840s, AND TRACES THE RISE OF MASS TOURISM IN THE SECOND HALF OF THE NINETEENTH CENTURY. LOCAL PEOPLE LIVING AROUND THE CAUSEWAY, MANY OF WHOSE FAMILIES WORKED AS BOATMEN AND GUIDES, CLAIM THAT IN THE NINETEENTH CENTURY THROUGH TO THE YEARS BETWEEN THE TWO WORLD WARS, THE SITE WAS ALMOST AS BUSY AS IT IS TODAY.

Visitors to the Giant's Causeway in the latter part of the eighteenth century, like tourists today, had three main requirements: accommodation, transport and the expectation of seeing something authentic, even unique. The ingenuity of local people met these needs and expectations with the provision of inns and hotels; transport in horse-drawn wagons, pony traps and small boats; the invention of one of the earliest hydroelectric trams; and the use of their natural wit and persuasion to enhance the visitors' experience of seeing the Giant's Causeway. Another motive was at work: to relieve the tourists of their cash.

Donal McCracken, reviewing the Georgian periods at the Causeway, wrote in the *Journal of the Glens of Antrim Historical Society* in 1985:

Notables were able to inflict themselves on the local gentry, but ordinary travellers were faced with a considerable problem. The two great hotels at the Causeway were products of the middle nineteenth century. Portrush was a little fishing village where in 1752 no lodgings were to be found.

Prior to 1806, there was no decent accommodation at Bushmills, the nearest village to the Causeway. McCracken concluded that the Georgian visitors:

... were never in number and mostly from the upper strata of society ... The Causeway was the preserve of the scientist, naturalist and romantic.

But all this was to change. Travellers in Ireland at this time began to write accounts of their adventures, and the travel book proliferated. As the number of visitors grew, guidebooks appeared in profusion – and, of course, with these came guides.

Wanderers such as the French emigrant Le Chevalier de la Tocnaye in 1796, and visitors from nearer areas, such as the Reverend Dr William Hamilton of Donegal in 1783-1784, often moved about on horseback. Both wrote lively accounts of their visits to the Causeway, the former in romantic terms and the latter with the sharp observational powers of the amateur naturalist. Anne Plumtree of Cambridge wrote of two summers' residence in Ireland, in 1814 and 1815. She took a guide from Ballintoy – about seven miles east of the

Right:
Sailing to the Causeway in 1900.
Left: A souvenir-seller at the Causeway's Wishing Chair in the late nineteenth century.

400/87 Portcoon Cave, Giant's Causeway

Boat trips into Portcoon Cave were once popular at the Causeway. The man on shore, with a bucket and long net, collected his tips after firing a gun to generate echoes around the cave.

Causeway – and walked to the famous site along the cliff-tops. Near Hamilton's Seat, she was intercepted by the Causeway guides:

... these men are like a parcel of hungry eagles, always hovering about, watching for prey, and the moment any is espied, the contest is commenced which can first pounce upon it.

William Thackeray expressed his own views about the boatmen-guides who, during his 1842 visit, bundled him into a boat much against his better judgement:

... for after all, it must be remembered it is pleasure we come for – that we are not obliged to take these boats. Well, well! I paid ten shillings for mine, and ten minutes before would cheerfully have paid five pounds to be allowed to quit it.

Another English visitor – Mrs Hall, touring Ireland with her husband in 1840 – had a more kindly view of the guides they encountered at popular sites. Mrs Hall says that the guides in Wicklow and Kerry '... delight in legends of fays and fairies, and they greet you with a jest and bid you farewell with a tear'. She described the northern guides at the Causeway as follows:

... of the earth – earthy; of the stone – stoney; they have the mystified look of philosophers, and the youngest and most ragged has a certain affection of learning that is very amusing. They are, however, attentive and obliging.

Who were these guides? Where did they live, and how did they operate?

John McConaghy, who in the 1960s was the National Trust's first warden at the Giant's Causeway, recorded his memories on audio tape in the 1950s:

I don't think now there are any boatmen, or combined boatmen-guides, at the Giant's Causeway. But in the old days – and I'm referring to the period before and after the First World War – there were dozens of them, and each man was a real character in his own right.

The guides lived in the various townlands and villages along the Causeway coast, and made a living from their activities during the tourist season. Boatmen were able to combine this with a bit of fishing, but the guides had to reap what they could in summer from the tourists. Edwin Waugh quoted a local woman's view of guiding in 1869:

The life o' a guide is a scattered thing ... in summer it's a' chops, an' steaks, an' mutton, an' tay, an' whiskey, an' when winter comes ... sleepin' an' shiverin' till the time gaes roun'.

Throughout the nineteenth century, a range of guidebooks to Ireland was available, and descriptions of facilities at the Giant's Causeway give a good idea of how accommodation and services had improved since the Georgian times.

During the 1830s, the Causeway Hotel, run by a Miss Henry, was established as an inn. Here in 1842, Thackeray, still uncomfortable from his boat ride, found sanctuary from the guides and had dinner and a good wine by a bright fire.

Baddeley's guidebook of 1887 lists the Causeway Hotel tariffs for boat trips with guides. Visitors were charged four shillings for 'the short course' and six shillings for 'the long course' (Thackeray was robbed when he was charged ten shillings almost fifty years earlier). The short trip included excursions into one or more of the nearby caves, then a voyage across the bay to the Causeway. The longer voyage also took in the superb scenery of the bays and headlands further east.

One 'entertainment' laid on to impress and amuse the boatloads of visitors took place at Portcoon Cave. Once inside, a boatman would give a signal, and an assistant – who had earlier been landed on a ledge at the mouth of the cave – would discharge a gun so that the clients could enjoy the echoes throughout the cave. The passengers' reactions varied, depending on whether or not they had been forewarned of this event. To receive his share of the takings, the gunner would reach out a long-handled fine net as the boats left the cave, at the same time hoping that the boatmen would remember him at the end of the day – for it was not unknown that he would be forgotten, left to languish on his cold perch while his colleagues drank their takings in the comfort of a hotel.

Much the same array of schemes and scams to relieve tourists of their cash existed at Killarney as at the Causeway, as is recorded on an annotated nineteenth-century postcard published by William Lawrence of Dublin:

Taste the mountain dew [probably whiskey or poteen], hear the wondrous echoes, buy bog oak and arbutus ornaments, and purchase photographs.

At the Causeway, as well as being offered the Portcoon experience, tourists were exposed to a hard sell on various specimens of minerals from the basalts, small representations of the Causeway carved from the stones, photographic albums of local scenes and, to accompany their drink of water from the Giant's Wishing Well, tots of Irish whiskey. A succession of elderly ladies worked their patch by a small spring at the Little Causeway, offering a cup of water and a wish to tourists. Some supplied whiskey, and some, of a more 'good-living' background, frowned on this practice and would not. Thackeray remarked of the whiskey-seller at the Causeway:

She has no change for a shilling: she never has; but her whiskey is good.

The specimens mentioned above included fossils. Although the Causeway rocks are volcanic and do not contain fossils, this was no deterrent to the initiative of the guides. They collected fossils at places such as White Park Bay and Kinbane Head, and, when demand outstripped supply, imported them from Devon. In winter, the guides were able to replenish their fossil stocks, but not without risk. Two guides were drowned off Ballintoy in 1894, during a boat trip to collect fossils at Kinbane Head, despite heroic efforts by coastguards and local fishermen to try and save them; the three other occupants of their boat were rescued.

In Esler's guidebook of 1884, there is the story in song of 'Little Irish Nell', who proffered specimens for sale at the Causeway. The song was written for a Miss Nelly Hayes, who performed it on stage:

Who'll buy a box of specimens just gathered from the strand?
I've Irish diamonds fit to deck the proudest in the land;

Alec McLernon (guide) and Mary Kane (water-provider) at the Wishing Well, Giant's Causeway, before the First World War.

With amethysts and jaspers too, that sparkle in the light,
And gems that glance like ladies' eyes, with lustre rare and bright.
The price is only half-a-crown, I really wish to sell;
Do buy a box of specimens from Little Irish Nell.

The boatmen took advantage of their captive audience to sell boxes of specimens. At some point in the journey, the oars would be shipped, and a box, wrapped in many layers of paper and bound with lots of string, was produced. The unwrapping took enough time for the sales pitch to reach full eloquence, and the customers perhaps had a feeling that a failure to purchase would delay their progress to the Causeway even further. Thackeray described this particular sales technique with some vehemence:

The boatmen insist upon you looking at boxes of 'specimens', which you must buy off them; they laugh as you grow paler and paler, they offer you more and more 'specimens'; even the lad who pulls number three, and is not allowed by his comrades to speak, puts in his oar, and hands you over a piece of Irish diamond ... and scorns you.

Boat trips were popular at the Causeway through to the inter-war years, as were excursions to and from the stones by pony and trap, up and down the road known as the 'quality rodden' (probably referring to the 'quality' people as patrons, rather than to the condition of the road, which was often in poor repair). But in the 1880s, a new invention added to the modes of transport available for getting visitors to the site.

The Causeway Tram

Child to Minister: *Did God make the tram?*

Minister: *Of course He did. Sure, didn't He make all creeping things!*

From 1887 to 1949, the Causeway tram creaked its way along the spectacular coastal route from Portrush to a terminus by the Causeway Hotel. Conceived and built by a local engineer, Dr William Traill, the tram drew its power from turbines at a mill on the River Bush, close to Bushmills. When it began running in 1883 (at this point it ran only to Bushmills; it was extended towards the Causeway four years later), it was the world's first commercially operated hydroelectric tram.

The tram became very popular with visitors and locals, although Traill had first intended it for transporting minerals. The railway from Belfast had reached Portrush in 1855, and a link was needed to the Causeway. For many years, horse-drawn carriages had ferried passengers to and from the Causeway; now there was a new and exciting form of transport.

In 1887, the tram carried 64,000 passengers. Its arrival in the grounds of the Causeway Hotel – which subsequently had the benefit of electric lighting from the same system – enabled the guides attached to this hotel to gain exclusive access to the passengers. Kane's Royal Hotel nearby, completed in 1876, was in competition with the Causeway Hotel, and attracted a number of guides who operated as 'outsiders' – freelancers of a sort. This advertisement was displayed locally by the Royal Hotel in 1890:

As the tram is in connection with the Causeway Hotel, and arrives in its grounds, the ROYAL HOTEL is looked upon as opposition, and is not allowed a Porter to represent it at the Tram Depot. A Porter from the Royal Arms Hotel, however, attends on the Public Road, which is the nearest way to the Giant's Causeway. Pay attention to his call; don't mind the Tram Touters.

An artistic impression of the Causeway Tram passing Dunluce Castle.

During a brief visit in 1876 by the Prince of Wales, later to become Edward VII, this distinguished visitor was given a cup of tea and he granted permission for the 'Royal' prefix.

At first, the Causeway tram drew its power from an electric rail which ran alongside the tracks at a low level. There was a certain naïveté about electricity in these early days, and William Traill, to demonstrate the rail's apparent safety to an inspector, dropped his trousers and sat on it. Only some time later did he admit to having received several painful shocks. The power line was later shifted to overhead wires.

During the Second World War, American servicemen arrived in Northern Ireland, providing welcome additional custom for the tram, which by then was beginning to suffer competition from motor cars. These soldiers, sailors and airmen spent their money on trips to see the Causeway; but they were the last boost to business, and the decision to close the tram was made at the end of 1949.

Today, there are few relics of the tram left. Stumps of the power poles survive along the road by Dunluce Castle, and two carriages, a saloon car and a partially open 'toast-rack' carriage, are preserved in the Ulster Folk and Transport Museum. The tram lives on in local memories, and its character has been caught in this extract from tram-enthusiast Brian McAlister's lament:

The saloon and toast-rack carriages of the Causeway Tram at the Causeway Hotel terminus, around 1900.

Out beyond the White Rocks,
Scootin' from Portrush,
Headin' for the Causeway,
Headin' for the Bush;
Watchin' from the Toast-rack
The hedge slippin' by,
Dizzy on the cliff-top-
Ye felt that high.
Scatterin' the seagulls
Round about Dunluce
Paddlin' through the fields again
Just like any goose;
Left behind by motor car,
Charabanc and bus,
Though ye whizzed an' clanged along,
Ratin' twenty plus.

The route of the Causeway tram – between Bushmills and Causeway Head, alongside the River Bush and across the Bushfoot sand dunes – is now a small railway, adding to the tourist attractions of the area.

Celebrities

Those of us who have worked at the Giant's Causeway in one capacity or another have encountered the famous and the notable, now labelled celebrities.

During a number of interviews the author carried out, unlocking the memories of a venerable third-generation Causeway guide, he asked him who, of the famous people he had met, made the most impression. His reply was surprising, and came without hesitation.

Not all of the famous, he admitted, arrive in a blaze of fuss and glory. Some slip in, are not recognised, and slip away again and it is only by chance one encounters them. Such a chance came one day, close to this guide's final retirement (he worked for a long time in his part-retirement doing various jobs about the Causeway). At the end of a tour, showing a small group of Americans around the site, he asked, as they stood on the famous stones, if any one of them had ever seen the likes of these rocks before. There was one response: a man at the back said quietly, 'Yes, up there,' jerking his head skyward. This guide had, that day, netted one of the rarest of the rare, one of the tiny band of human beings who had walked on the moon.

Americans at the Causeway

The logbooks kept by guides in the nineteenth century were signed by many visitors, who endorsed their individual guide's qualities and possibly added some humorous comments or a few lines of verse. Records from two surviving logbooks, covering the 1860s and 1870s, show numerous entries by Americans hailing from New York across to California, although the eastern and central states and cities predominate. Visitors from New York, Boston, Philadelphia, Cincinnati and Chicago (and many from Canada, too) enjoyed the wit and company of Causeway guides such as John MacLaughlin and James Hutchinson, and many others. Resident expatriates praised the Causeway, and no doubt their recommendations added to the flow of American visitors:

Christmas 1869. Edw. D. Neill, Consul, U.S. of America at Dublin, found the guide an intelligent expounder of the geologic structure of the peculiar finger work of God, called the Giant's Causeway.

Traffic between the United States and the Giant's Causeway was not all one way. The basalt columns, sometimes in considerable numbers, also travelled, as detailed in the next chapter.

CARING FOR THE CAUSEWAY
From Exploitation to Conservation

THE CONCEPTS OF PROTECTION AND CONSERVATION WERE INTRODUCED AT THE GIANT'S CAUSEWAY IN 1961, WHEN THE NATIONAL TRUST ACQUIRED THE SITE. IN THE TWENTY-FIRST CENTURY, MUCH EFFORT AND EXPERTISE IS EXPENDED TO TRY AND BALANCE THE INCREASING VISITOR NUMBERS WITH LANDSCAPE AND NATURE CONSERVATION. TO UNDERSTAND THE NEED FOR THESE, IT IS NECESSARY TO RETRACE THE CAUSEWAY'S HISTORY, SELECTING RELEVANT EVENTS FROM THE PAST.

Blood from the Stones

Stephen Gwynn, in *Highways and Byways of Donegal and Antrim* (1899), described how he arrived at the Causeway in 1898 to find it:

... tourist-ridden with a vengeance. Besides, a company has enclosed it with a railing, and makes visitors pay sixpence for admission — an innovation started Easter Monday of this year, which every good Irishman resents.

Changes in ownership of the Giant's Causeway, plus its increasing popularity as a tourist destination through the nineteenth century, contributed to the almost inevitable development of commercial exploitation. The Causeway and surrounding areas were part of lands that came by royal grant in the early seventeenth century to the Earl of Antrim and retained over successive generations. The Causeway and its surroundings were leased to a John McCollum as a fee-farm grant in 1738, and in 1796 the site passed, through marriage, to the Lecky family. There was, however, confusion over details of the leasing arrangements, and the Antrim lessors disputed points of ownership over many years. In 1863, the Leckys erected a two-storey caretaker's house on the very edge of the Grand Causeway, involving the destruction of columns on the west side of this feature. This damage added to that caused by years of quarrying of the stones for sale as curios and souvenirs, as remembered on audio-tape by John McConaghy in the 1950s (who, a decade later, found himself charged with the Causeway's protection when he was employed by the National Trust):

I'd like to mention the fact that in my days, the boxing of Giant's Causeway pillars was quite an industry. The guides and boatmen used to quarry these pillars and box them and send them off to Australia and Canada and the United States of America.

These travelling columns, like earlier human emigrants, found their way to the USA, and to some other rather unusual places. A story still circulating in the 1980s told of a number of columns from the Causeway being taken to Philadlephia and erected there in a public park. This no doubt originated in the 1907 scandal that the entire Causeway was destined for America, reported in the *Northern Whig* and *Coleraine Constitution* newspapers and even reaching such worthy papers as the *Manchester Guardian* and *New York Times*. The fact that it remains *in situ* today is evidence of confusion in 1907 – it was the Causeway Columnar Basalt Company (perhaps an unwise choice of name) that was looking into sending basalt aggregate to the USA from its inland quarries. President John F. Kennedy took home a piece of Causeway column, presented to him during his visit to the Republic of Ireland in June 1963; a column ended up at the Hibernian Society in Charleston, South Carolina in 1851; two pieces of a column are underneath the streets of Twickenham in London, acquired by the poet Alexander Pope from an influential friend and placed in a grotto he maintained for such curiosities, and of course many samples have ended up in museums around the world. A few have been used as gravestones, and one piece of a Causeway column sailed into war in the Falklands on board HMS *Antrim*. Finally, an amusing incident worth recording: a group of extremely realistic full-size columns was constructed from polystyrene and painted very accurately – even including lichens – for a television advert in the 1990s. These proved

Access to the Giant's Causeway was fenced off (close to the house) from about 1898 to about 1961.

useful afterwards for taking along to school talks and other functions. They were set down on the Causeway for a publicity stunt one day, and a member of staff, carrying the last one up the hill from the site, was accosted by a large American gentleman on his way down to view the famous stones. 'Hey, buddy, I do believe you're not allowed to remove these precious things from here.' It did not seem to occur to him that such a block would have weighed close to one tonne. Some columns are as widely travelled as those who come to see them!

Don't Fence Me In

Towards the end of the nineteenth century, the Causeway was becoming very busy. In 1896, the Causeway Tram carried 100,000 visitors to the site and many others arrived by various other means. In that year, the Leckys leased the Causeway to a private syndicate called the Giant's Causeway Company who declared their intention to enclose the famous stones and charge admission. After two hundred years of free public access, this understandably caused considerable protest, with much coverage in local, regional and national press. A committee to defend the Causeway was formed, and in March 1897, the case came to court in Dublin.

This was an interesting case in Irish Property Law, the division of Ireland between the Irish Free State (now the Republic of Ireland) and Northern Ireland not being officially proclaimed until 1922. The defendants – the committee – challenged the Leckys' ownership, maintained that there were public rights of way to and across the Causeway stones, and insisted that that there were long-standing local customary rights to use and enjoy various features of the site.

Much evidence to support the defendants' case was sought. Maps, Vivarès' engravings of Susanna Drury's 1739 paintings of the Causeway and older illustrations, were produced to support the long history of public interest and use, and to show that paths existed from the public road to the Causeway. Some of this evidence was rejected as inadmissible. Guides and other locals were cross-examined in court. George Kane-Smith, whose family built and owned the former Kane's Royal Hotel, described his great-grandmother Mary Jane Kane, a formidable lady, being called to give evidence (G. Kane-Smith, 2011). However, the judge, finding for the plaintiffs, upheld the Leckys' right to ownership, concluded that there was no declared intention to create public rights of way, nor was there a proven right to wander at will over the Causeway. The Giant's Causeway Company was therefore able to pursue its intentions. An appeal followed, but also failed. On April 16, 1898 – Easter Monday – the new arrangements for charging and admission commenced, under the administration of the syndicate.

Golden Years

Enclosure did not diminish the tourist numbers. The first motor car arrived at the Causeway in 1910, and the site remained a popular place to visit throughout the First World War (1914-1918). The 1920s and 1930s – the inter-war years

Early motor cars at the Causeway Hotel. Both hotels were owned by Kane from 1910 to 1963.

– were a 'golden age' at the Giant's Causeway: this feeling is still strong in living memories amongst the local communities. At this time, both large hotels were flourishing; guides and boatmen were in full swing; tram-loads of visitors arrived regularly and the small shops and tearooms along the Causeway bays did a strong, if seasonal, trade. A travelling community, arriving at Easter and leaving at the end of September, provided visitors with additional entertainments, from fortune-telling to harmonica-playing.

During the Second World War (1939-1945), the Royal Hotel remained open, while troops were billeted at the Causeway Hotel; but soon this strongly commercialised age began to wane, the Causeway Tram ceased operations in 1949 and by the 1950s the numbers of guides had decreased. Another change was in the air.

End of an Era

In 1961, the Giant's Causeway was transferred from private to public ownership, and the emphasis began to shift from commercialisation to conservation.

The National Trust, founded in 1895 as a voluntary organisation (now a registered charity) dedicated to the preservation of places of historic interest or natural beauty, secured an option in 1960 to purchase the assets of the Giant's Causeway Company, as well as the freehold interests of the Lecky family. Lord Antrim, chairman of the National Trust's Committee in Northern Ireland at this time, continued his family's interest in the Giant's Causeway: he encouraged the necessary purchases, in 1961 and 1962, which brought the Causeway, and surrounding bays and headlands, into the ownership of an organisation with the right to declare its properties inalienable – in other words, once so declared they can not be sold except by parliamentary consent. This is a powerful and long-term way of holding sites for the benefit of present and future generations. Further lands along the cliff tops were acquired from Sir Anthony Macnaghten of Bushmills.

The Trust set about tidying up the approaches to the Causeway. The turnstile and railings were pulled out, admission charges ceased, and gradually all of the surviving shops and other buildings were removed (some retained their businesses in kiosks at a site behind the cliff-tops at Causeway Head). The Trust established its own tearoom and a small information point by the car park close to the public road, but never intended to remove visitor services entirely. It was thought desirable, and in keeping with efforts to return the Causeway's immediate environment to as natural a condition as possible, to move the services in the bays to a less intrusive location.

Not unnaturally, there was some resentment of this on the part of former Causeway traders, who felt that all these conservation ideals harmed their ability to make their living. There were new opportunities for employment, however, as the Trust took on staff to repair and extend footpaths and to serve the public in the tearoom and information building, and they appointed their first warden in 1967.

Fresh Air and Exercise

The spectacular coastline which spreads out east and west of the Giant's Causeway was increasingly realised to be a great natural asset, offering opportunities for superb walks. Nevertheless, natural erosion and earlier quarrying and path cutting had caused damage, with areas of loose rocks and stones and dangerous gaps and overhangs below the cliffs. Add these to the changeable Atlantic weather, the high cliffs and local landowners' concerns about people crossing their land, it became obvious that maintaining safe public access was a challenge. It was also important to avoid disturbing plants, birds and other wildlife.

As boat trips had ceased, there was an urgent need to improve coastal paths. In 1964, following purchases, covenants and other agreements between the National Trust, local authorities and various landowners, sixteen kilometres (ten miles) of cliff-top path from Runkerry to Dunseverick Castle were declared open to the public. Between 1968 and 1978, various work schemes supported by employment agencies enabled the Trust, taking on local people with the necessary skills, to improve this coastal path network on both the cliff-tops and down to sea level.

What the Visitors Want

In 1980, the Northern Ireland Tourist Board carried out a survey of visitors to the Giant's Causeway. The 'Troubles' in Northern Ireland (1969–1994) certainly affected tourist numbers in the Province, and there was a real fear of coming to the Six Counties – a fear that was proving difficult to overcome for those promoting a region whose positive aspects such as the beauties of the coast and countryside and the friendliness of the people were regularly undermined by alarming news headlines.

Throughout the Troubles, the Giant's Causeway remained a strong attraction to visitors who were not put off by bad news, and the famous stones became, more than ever, an icon which the tourism industry used to sell Northern Ireland as a destination in these difficult times. The north Antrim coast, while not escaping terrorism completely, offered a haven for the day tripper as well as for the tourist. Journalists and other media representatives from all over the world, in the Province to cover stories on the political and civil unrest, almost always took a trip to see the Causeway; and therein lay wonderful opportunities to communicate – for free – the better side of life in Northern Ireland, opportunities that were well utilised up to and after the 1994 IRA (Irish Republican Army) ceasefire.

The 1980 survey showed that visitors were, on the whole, reasonably satisfied with the Giant's Causeway. When asked what they might like to see in a visitor centre if one was provided, they showed strong preferences for legends, folklore, crafts, geology and details of the Spanish Armada *Girona* shipwreck. There was also an interest in finding out more about the local flora and fauna.

The 1980s saw many changes at the Giant's Causeway and its surroundings. On the cliff-top, beside the Causeway Hotel (Kane's Royal Hotel was demolished by a new owner in 1963), the National Trust in partnership with the local authority Moyle District Council, created a substantial new visitor centre, the first of its kind on the site and complete with the latest interpretive information, shops and a cafe. This centre opened in May 1986, won many awards and serviced the increasing numbers of visitors now encouraged to come to the Province in more peaceful times. A small minibus assisted access to the Giant's Causeway and in 1995 a new and expanded bus shuttle service commenced, and is still running today.

As emphasised in the Introduction, in 1986 the Giant's Causeway, including 71 hectares of the surrounding coastline from Port-na-boe below the visitor centre east to Benbane Head, was added to the UNESCO World Heritage list. It is within the natural sites category, selected largely because it exhibits geological and landscape features of global importance and contributes to our understanding of an important period in the Earth's physical history. Acknowledgement is also given to the cultural value of the nearby *Girona* Spanish Armada wreck location. To date (2012), this remains Northern Ireland's only World Heritage Site.

The same area was declared a National Nature Reserve by the Northern Ireland Department of the Environment in 1987, emphasising both its geological and wildlife importance. In 1989, this organisation included the Causeway within its declared Causeway Coast Area of Outstanding Natural Beauty. Explanations of such designations are given in Appendix One.

Thus, by the end of the 1980s, the Giant's Causeway had many official decorations to add to its natural beauty. What advantages did all these bring to the site and its owners, managers and neighbours? The designations carry some weight when help is sought in financing the care and running of the Giant's Causeway and its services, with the provision of educational, interpretive and promotional materials and they offer some safeguards (not always fully effective) when planning issues arise along the designated coastal strip. With the Causeway as the 'honeypot' centrally placed on a beautiful coastline, and many people coming to enjoy the scenery, there has been a continuing expansion in the development of hotels, bed and breakfast establishments and holiday homes, as well as other amenities, all contributing to the local economy. It's nice to have letters after your name, but it is better if they do you some good.

To the Millenium and Beyond

As the 1990s progressed, nobody knew, despite much speculation, what the approaching new millennium would bring. At the Giant's Causeway, and all along the Causeway Coast, visitor numbers continued to rise, and popular sites such as the Causeway, some of the beautiful beaches and the Carrick-a-Rede rope bridge began to feel the pressure of numbers, particular in the summer months and when good weather prevailed, bringing people outdoors. Northern Ireland has for many decades been a car-dominated culture, and the provision of adequate parking and alternative public transport are two issues still relevant on this coastline.

A major landslip in December 1993 on the lower coastal path in the Amphitheatre, a little east of the Giant's Causeway, caused a temporary closure while the National Trust engaged experts to look at the geological, conservation and access issues brought about by this and other slips and rock falls. Engineers were consulted to ascertain if the risk factors could be reduced by physical intervention where weakness in the cliffs and slopes existed. It was finally concluded, after consultations with UNESCO (World Heritage Site) that the path should be closed permanently and that natural processes should be allowed to proceed. The path from the entrance to the Amphitheatre to Hamilton's Seat was permanently closed in June 1994. Much more of it has slipped or become vegetated and it is now (2012) much less obvious than it was two decades ago and an extremely hazardous area, to be avoided by all except a few specialists authorised now and then to venture along it for inspections.

Considering the period 2000-2017, tourism is now a major economic factor, and on the north coast it affects all communities, from Derry City to Rathlin Island. Commercial fishing for salmon has gone through a steady decline and conservation measures have further reduced fishing activities while sport angling, in river, lake and at sea, has been promoted, mining has long since ceased, quarrying is limited and agriculture, while remaining important, has had to adapt to European influences and dynamic weather patterns perhaps influenced by global warming. Golf and sea sports, notably surfing, have become major leisure activities. More people are enjoying exploring the coast by walking and on the cycling routes that are now available.

One could ask if all this is for the good, or are the popular sites in particular, and the coast in general, at risk of becoming as exploited as the Giant's Causeway was in the past? All of the above points link to the main challenge facing conservation organisations and relevant government departments that own or otherwise manage many sites such as beaches, cliffs, even islands, alongside the privately owned farms and estates. It also takes a good working partnership to provide access. The question facing all is: how to protect and conserve the outstanding natural beauty of the area, its internationally important geology and diverse wildlife while coping with the rising tide of visitors, whether day trippers or tourists, holiday home occupiers, caravan enthusiasts or whoever, and also enable residents make a reasonable living from various businesses and occupations? What happens at the Giant's Causeway is relevant to everything.

In April 2000, the Giant's Causeway Visitor Centre was destroyed in a fire, not a good opening to the new millennium. However, temporary facilities were quickly put in place and after a long period of discussion by decision makers, eventually plans were approved for a new visitor centre. An advantage of the protracted period of "temporary' facilities was the chance for wide consultation and considerable thought into provisioning the needs of residents, visitors and the natural environment. One result is the new centre, which opened in summer 2012, built and fitted with the latest in environmentally friendly technology, carefully placed into the contours of the cliff-top topography and kitted out with modern interpretive features, shops, restaurant and other facilities. It is hoped that the substantial cost of creating this new centre, although grant-aided, will be offset by a high level of visitor participation.

The visitor numbers at the Giant's Causeway are already (2012) around 750,000 per annum, and, as stated in the introduction, are anticipated to reach one million per year in the present decade. Apart from seeing the extraordinary Causeway stones, and marvelling at the dramatic scenery, how many visitors will consider the rare narrow-mouthed whorl snail, notice the pink and white flowers of the scarce mountain everlasting (also known as catspaw), ever see the light-bulb sea squirt or realise that up to twenty-five different habitats support a wide range of plants, insects, birds and other wildlife within a short distance of the famous stones?

From Stones to Snails

The flora and fauna of the Giant's Causeway and its bays, cliffs and headlands comprises more that you might expect from an exposed north-facing Atlantic coastline. The ocean and its underwater environment are discussed in the next chapter.

Between the cliff-top farmlands and the sea are various types of heath, both dry and wet, marshes and other damp habitats, cliffs, grassy and often shady slopes, areas of loose stones known as scree, salt-marsh and rocky shores. Even on the much tramped Causeway stones, low clumps of wild flowers find nooks and crannies to put down roots. In spring and early summer, the slopes and cliff tops are natural rockeries of colourful flora, from primroses and violets to masses of sea pink and taller red campion and many more, including rare and scarce species such as the oyster plant and Scots lovage. Bees, hoverflies, moths and butterflies visit these to feed and some to lay eggs, and the more obvious birds include singing skylarks and the cackling fulmars on their cliff breeding sites. The rare red-legged crow known as the chough has gone from the area although a pair currently breeds on Rathlin Island and hope is maintained that they might return to the Causeway cliffs, where farm management includes maintaining short grasslands which these birds favour as feeding areas. The rare twite, a small brown finch, is still found within the World Heritage Site and the retention of winter cereal stubble provides feeding for these and flocks of other

National Trust workers maintaining the Causeway Coast path in the 1980s.

small birds. Nature conservation at the Causeway is a year-round activity, and includes the control and management of invading scrub and rank grasslands. It is difficult to use grazing stock (sheep, cattle and horses), as found at some nature reserves, to manage vegetation in a site with so many human visitors.

Naturalists have been active along this north coast mainly since the eighteenth century, some chipping at rocks, others bent over peering at flowers, a few collecting tiny snails and the like and more watching birds. These were – and sometimes still are – regarded by some locals as strange behaviours, and in the past a few wondered at the sanity of these early nature enthusiasts. However, it was not until the flourishing of field clubs and other natural history societies in the mid to late nineteenth century that information began to be gathered in more detail. Now, professional and amateur geologists and biologists and general naturalists abound, and much more is known and being added to the now computer-organised data-bases on Ulster's natural history, the Giant's Causeway included.

In 1977 and 1978, surveys were carried out along the north coast to record breeding bird communities and look at how these might be spared too much disturbance by tourists and others. Biological surveys of National Trust properties, including the Giant's Causeway and other north coast sites, were completed in 1985, 1992 and 2004. Universities and other organisations also carried out relevant specialist investigations of lichens, flowering plants, mammals and birds, to name just a few. Chapter 8 provides more details.

Site managers' shelves now creak with the weight of reports, surveys, management plans and so on; staff at desks collating and recording all this data on computers may wish they were out on fieldwork; the various designating bodies require evidence of good management, and residents and visitors want to get out and enjoy the scenery, and see examples of the wildlife spectacles they are now used to viewing on television.

Some of the solutions to balancing human access to the coast and countryside and caring for landscape and wildlife are already being implemented: provision and maintenance of good paths, clear signage, promotion of health and safety issues, employment of rangers and guides and increasing support from volunteers, protection and monitoring of fragile habitats and their flora and fauna. The Giant's Causeway Visitor Centre, owned and run by the National Trust, together with their scientific, wardening and educational staff based nearby, comprise the hub of conservation activities in the area. Information is constantly up-dated by surveys and contract-based research. Thus the quality of habitats and the flora and fauna these support are monitored and protected.

Above: *A grey seal uses its sharp claws to cling to a rock.*

Right: *Red campion is a vigorous plant which flowers along this coastline in spring and summer. Here it forms a thick clump under a laterite exposure in one of the Causeway bays.*

Above: An Easter snowfall turns spring back to winter for these cattle, which are more interested in finding food than in the view of Rathlin Island, in the east, and of the Mull of Kintyre in Scotland.

Below: The guesthouses of the popular holiday resort of Portrush cluster along the neck of the volcanic sill of Ramore Head.

Above: *Shallow water; the grass-capped, eroded coves, caves and arches of the White Rocks near Portrush; and dark volcanic basalt behind.*

Below: *Male and female eiders coming in to land.*

Above: The dramatic remains of Dunluce Castle. The shell of the Jacobean manor house dominates the centre of the site, while the eroded cliff in the foreground is a reminder of a stormy evening in 1639 when the kitchen collapsed into the sea, taking several servants to their deaths.

Below: Irish hares sporting.

Opposite: A precarious rope bridge slung across the neck of an extinct volcano at Carrick-a-Rede. In the past the original rope bridge gave fishermen access to their nets, but the fishery is now closed. A new bridge provides a thrill for the thousands of tourists who venture over it each summer.

Above: *Kinbane Castle – a hidden gem tucked away in a remote cove at the eastern end of the Causeway Coast.*

Below: *The shag, or green cormorant, nests on ledges and in caves along the Causeway Coast, often decorating its nest with colourful bits of fishing-net and rope.*

Opposite: *Portaneevey viewpoint is one of the few places on the mainland from which the now-abandoned salmon fishery of Carrick-a-Rede can be spotted. This photo was taken when the bag net still operated.*

Above: Treasure recovered from the wreck of the Spanish Armada ship Girona.

Left: Kelp and a grazing sea urchin (centre).

A Dynamic Coastline

Change, however, is a certainty as inevitable as death and taxes. This is a dynamic coastline – the scars of landslips and rock-falls can be seen at many places in the bays and on the slopes and cliffs and even underwater. Erosion and weathering of the landscape by natural forces and human pressures continues. Some of these changes benefit wildlife by providing new habitats and opportunities for colonising, or re-colonising, various sites. However, the possible, indeed likely, effects of climate change also have to be considered.

One of the most discussed effects of a warming global climate is the rise of sea level. Various projections have been put forward, but few scientists doubt there will be a significant increase in sea level by the end of the twenty-first century.

In 2006, the National Trust commissioned a team of university specialists to investigate how the climate of Northern Ireland is likely to change during this century, how these changes might impact on sites such as the Giant's Causeway and what might be done to cope with these challenges. A detailed report was produced and a summary, entitled *Shifting Shores*, was published by the Trust in 2007.

The Giant's Causeway World Heritage Site is likely to be affected by more extreme weather, including storms and storm surges and inundation by large waves, higher tides and a rising sea level. Coastal erosion will increase and flora and fauna may suffer habitat change and loss. In the longer term, parts of the Causeway promontories may be intermittently or fully submerged. Apart from the effects on the landscape and its wildlife, these changes may provide challenges for human access and the overall management of the area. In a broader context, it will boil down to trying to hold the line or adapting, depending a lot on whether the affected coastal sites are soft, for example low-lying sandy shores or mudflats backed by farmland or centres of occupation, or hard, such as the mainly cliff-bound Causeway Coast. Change will come, and it is sound sense to be prepared.

Whatever the sea level, it should not be overlooked that the Giant's Causeway is in every sense a signpost to the ocean and what lies below.

Rock-fall on the cliff path.

SHORE, SEA AND SHIPWRECKS
Above and Below the Waves

A T THE GIANT'S CAUSEWAY ON A ROUGH DAY, THE SEA, OR RATHER, THE ATLANTIC OCEAN, MAKES ITS PRESENCE FELT IN NO UNCERTAIN TERMS. GREEN WAVES TOPPED WITH WHITE FOAM CRASH OVER THE COLUMNS, SPRAY FLIES IN THE AIR, SENSIBLE PEOPLE STAND WELL BACK AND STILL FEEL DROPLETS OF WATER ON THEIR FACE, TASTE THE SALT, SMELL THE OCEAN TANG, SEE AND HEAR THE NEXT BREAKER ROLLING AND ROARING IN TOWARDS THEM. EVEN IN CALM WEATHER, THE OCEAN SENDS SMALL WAVELETS RUNNING UP THE SHORE TO SUCK HUNGRILY AT THEIR FEET; IT IS A RARE DAY WHEN IT IS FLAT CALM, AND THEN NEVER FOR LONG. OVER HUNDREDS OF YEARS, MARINERS HAVE LEARNED TO RESPECT THIS COASTLINE AND ITS OCEAN AND NUMEROUS SHIPWRECK SITES ARE REMINDERS OF THE CHANGEABLE NATURE OF WEATHER AND SEA CONDITIONS AND THE PRESENCE OF DANGEROUS REEFS.

Through many millennia, sea levels have risen and fallen, and for equally lengthy periods the tide has come in and gone out twice every twenty-four hours. Beyond the shores, the sea is not a featureless expanse of water but is as complex as the land and often supports a greater diversity of life than on even the richest of terrestrial nature reserves. Marine biologists and ocean scientists have a complex terminology that classifies the various zones from the tide line to the deeps, and what follows is an attempt to present these for the Causeway Coast's shoreline, inshore and offshore waters in a condensed and simplified form. In this chapter, we explore first the seashore exposed at low tide, then move out gradually through the shallows to deeper water. Fascinating new information from multi-beam SONAR (SOund Navigation And Ranging) and sub-aqua diving surveys over the past decade provides details of the seabed off the Causeway Coast, and what lives there.

Life in the water itself, from tiny drifting and swimming plankton (plants and animals) to fish and larger creatures such as whales, dolphins and the basking shark, is visited later. Some seabirds are truly marine animals, spending all of their lives out on the oceans except for a few months when they must come ashore to breed. The Causeway Coast and Rathlin Island, in particular, support many seabirds, some oceanic, others more coastal, and it is also worth taking them into consideration.

The broadest definition of this marine environment is to divide it into two major areas: between the tides and beyond the tides. The latter is more complex and the former more accessible.

Between the Tides
Relaxing on a beach, finding just the right sort of sand for sandcastles, beachcombing for interesting things washed ashore, eating gritty sandwiches (how appropriate this word is), pottering about rock pools with nets and buckets – many of us enjoy these simple seaside pleasures as children, adults and then, if we are especially graced, with our grandchildren.

One of the major attractions of the Causeway Coast is its variety of shorelines, from sandy beaches to rocky platforms – many with pools filled with sea life – and the more exposed shores of bedrock, boulders and sea cliffs where, here and there, small coves exist that are so remote only the sea kayaker or small boat enthusiast finds them. This coast and its hinterland has been deservedly designated an Area of Outstanding Natural Beauty (AONB, see Appendix One), or should that be Area Of Nets and Buckets?

The relentless rise and fall of the tides cover then expose what is known as the inter-tidal or littoral zone. Most of us who are not trained sub-aqua divers must wait for the receding tide to allow us dip into the delights of life on the shore. Such things there are to find! Slippery little green blennies (fish), some in rock pools, others living under moist seaweed and able to absorb enough

Kelp at low tide.

oxygen to survive till the tide comes in again; nippers and creepers like lobsters, squat lobsters and various crabs; shrimps and rock prawns that dart and flicker in the pools; beautiful sea anemones, some with waving feeder tentacles, others with these withdrawn and like a blob of jelly; shells of various shapes and hues, some maybe containing a hermit crab; if really lucky, a colourful sea slug with waving 'skirts' and much more. Bring a good guide to seashore life with your nets and buckets, and wear something on your feet – rocks can be sharp and a nip by a crab or the jab of a sea urchin spine can be painful. Always remember to replace any rocks or seaweed shifted in your searches, for the creatures underneath do not appreciate the hot sun or the cold eye of a hungry gull.

Life between the tides can be tough. When you depend on seawater as your life support system, it is a bit inconvenient when it disappears for a few hours twice a day. The plants and animals of the littoral zone have adapted in many ways to these variations.

There are many types of seaweed, which are not in fact weeds but algae, from pale green lettuce-leaf types, while more emerald species on some rocky areas usually indicate the influence of some fresh water, to various red algae, some of which grow on the stalks of the large brown leathery species that are part of the loose grouping known as kelp. There is an interesting zonation of these algae from the upper to the lower shore and beyond: those highest on the shore have the longest exposure to the air and consequently can withstand being partly dried, the middle shore has more slippery brown and red algae that can have small sacs filled with air that help them float when the tide comes in (such as bladder wrack) or are rather flattened with ragged edges (saw wrack), and low on the shore are large flopped-over broad brown algae such as oarweed – the stalks (stipes) and fronds glisten and feel slimy, and in the deeper water just beyond the tides they wave to and fro in the swell. Seen underwater, the tallest of these form dense 'forests' and extend into deeper water as far as light penetrates, for they, like land plants, must use the energy of sunlight to nurture themselves.

Thus plants and animals of the inter-tidal area face the hazards of drying out, sometimes pollution from the land, in the form of run-off of fertilisers from agricultural fields or sewage, changes the salinity (saltiness) of what water there is – in hot weather evaporation can makes pools saltier and rain or seepage of freshwater can reduce salinity, and there are predators stalking about, from the occasional heron ready to stab a fish to hungry gulls and the chisel-beaked oystercatcher which, despite its name, loves mussels and limpets which it can prize from the rocks or chip into with its red beak. Limpets clamp down tight on rocks to retain moisture, and some fish, such as the above-mentioned blennies, as well as rocklings and pipefishes, can exist in the moist coolness under seaweeds or in rock pools. Then in comes the tide, the water is back, but strong wave action can dislodge algae and disturb animals. A new set of predators may arrive, such as the creeping killer octopus, and large crabs and lobsters emerge from their hiding places to grab and crush and tear whatever is within reach. There is a small marine snail called the netted dog whelk that can bore a hole into shellfish such as limpets to get at the flesh. Who'd be a limpet, you might ask, with so many challenges to what otherwise seems a quiet life.

Some of the best sites for shore exploration are the rocky platforms from Portstewart to Portballintrae, the gently sloping rock and boulder shores in the Causeway bays, the pools and low reefs around Ballintoy Harbour and along this shore towards Whitepark Bay and the rocky coves and pools around Dunseverick Harbour. Rathlin Island has a mainly cliff-bound coast, but where there are accessible rocky shores there is much to be found – this island's marine environment comprises one of the richest sea sites in Ireland. Islands and other offshore areas are discussed further into this chapter.

There are no muddy shores along this coast, except within estuaries at the River Bann and Lough Foyle. These are the best locations to see wading birds and wildfowl, but along the Causeway Coast's beaches and rocky areas are shorebirds such as ringed plovers, sanderlings, redshanks, curlews, turnstones, oystercatchers, rock pipits and, on the cliffs in spring and summer, breeding seabirds, more of which later. The occasional peregrine falcon and buzzard may be spotted, or heard, the former with shrill cries and the latter mewing like a cat.

Finally, a few words about tides, as these are worth keeping an eye on, whether exploring the shoreline or getting out on the water surfing, kayaking or otherwise boating. The tidal range – the height between low tide and high tide – is relatively low on this coast. The maximum is 2 metres at Magilligan in County Londonderry and 1 metre at the other end of the coast at Ballycastle in County Antrim (measured at spring tides when the rise and fall is greatest). Around the Giant's Causeway, the range is about 1.5 metres. Conversely, tidal current are strong and rip currents occur at rocky headlands and off beaches, notably at Whitepark Bay. Large waves occur frequently, mostly in windy weather, but even on a still day a big swell can send breakers foaming up the shore. A set of tide tables is useful as is a healthy dose of common sense and both might mean avoiding a call to the Coastguards.

Beyond the Tides

The oceans and seas cover seven tenths (almost three-quarters) of our globe. The Atlantic Ocean meets the North Channel (itself leading into the Irish Sea) off the Causeway Coast. Referring to recent sea-bed research outlined above, the edge of the sea just beyond the lowest of low tides is considered first, then the shallows out to somewhat deeper water, looking at both sea-bed structure and also what lives there. Following this is a short account of the open sea and ocean, taking in the layers from the air above the waves to the sea surface and down through the water column to near the sea bed.

Underwater is a fascinating and life-filled space that many of us never experience first-hand, so let us follow the divers and glimpse the riches that exist beyond the Giant's Causeway's shores.

Over your Wellies – the Sub-Littoral Fringe

The edge of the sea that lies just beyond the lowest of low tides is known as the sub-littoral fringe. It may be a gentle slope into this area, a sudden seepage over the top of your boots, or it can be a steep drop into underwater kelp forests of red and brown algae. On a sandy beach, it's the bit you worry about when the kids get very wet. One way it can be explored is by snorkelling – preferably

Northern starfish, Lepasterias muelleri.

protected from the cold by a wet-suit.

The greatest variety of plants and animals is usually found on the rocky part of this zone, although mud and sand can contain large numbers of small creatures from tiny snails to various types of worms living amongst these sediments. You only have to see the abundant curly casts of lugworms on wet sand between the tides to get a clue to such shore life under your feet, and it's much the same in inshore and offshore areas.

The clear waters off the Causeway Coast permit good light penetration, and large algae such as in the kelp forests can exist down to depths of 20 metres, for example on rocky areas off Benbane Head and even deeper off Rathlin Island. These big brown seaweeds are particularly thick along this fringe just beyond the tidal zone as long as there are sufficient rocky or boulder and stony areas for the algae to anchor themselves by tangled root-like holdfasts. The flexible stipes (stalks) and pliable fronds like broad brown leaves are able to withstand the surge of normal waves and currents, but in winter they decay somewhat, are weakened by wave shock and large banks of them are washed ashore by winds and big swells. Attached to these large algae are smaller seaweeds, often beautifully coloured from pink and red to deep claret and purple. Some, like the leaf-like dulse, are edible: dulse is collected, dried in the sun and sold at various sites around this coast. It is slightly salty, chewy and has a tang of iodine – good for you if you can get it down.

Seals and fish cruise through these kelp forests, or kelp parks as they are sometimes called. Occasionally, an otter will venture from land into this fish-rich fringe, to come ashore with perhaps a colourful wrasse which it will chomp to pieces while sitting on a seaweed-covered rock – a sight worth seeing. Some birds dive amongst the kelp to seek food, including the cormorant, shag and eider duck. Purple and pink common sea urchins graze (rasp would be a better description) on the algae fronds, as do many other, smaller creatures. Tiny blue-rayed limpets browse on the broad fronds through the summer and many do not survive their first year. There is a sub-species of this little limpet that is a little cleverer – prior to the winter deterioration of the seaweed they migrate to the holdfast at the base of the plant, excavate a hollow and continue to live through the winter. You can sometimes find both the smaller and more brightly marked ones on the fronds of kelp washed ashore, and it's worth looking in the tangled holdfast for the slightly larger and duller older form of this amazing creature. There are many complex relationships and stories that could be told of life in the sea.

In summer, lobsters and large brown or edible crabs move into this inshore fringe and lurk in crevices or move about in the shelter of seaweeds or rocks. They may sometimes be found by divers, or caught by fishermen able to set creels very close in during calmer weather. A big swell would wreck and tangle and scatter their gear, so it is a brief spell during which they can fish the fringe. Stormy weather exerts considerable wave surge and shock in this exposed zone, making it an area where life can at times be difficult – anyone searching through the kelp washed ashore – as many birds do – will find a range of marine creatures stranded or dead.

Over your Head – the Sub-Littoral Zone

Although the sub-littoral fringe can vary from boot-filling shallows to several metres in depth, in the true sub-littoral area you are well out of your depth. Exploration includes techniques such as snorkelling, sub-aqua diving (normal limit is around 50 metres), sampling with grabs, dredges and the like, or, less damaging, by scanning with underwater video and other camera-based viewing, some attached to Remote Underwater Vehicles (ROVs) that can penetrate much deeper than any diver. It is the main zone off the Causeway Coast, extending out for several kilometres and down to depths beyond 50 metres. The very deep water off the north-west end of Rathlin Island, as much as 224 metres (730 feet), is close enough to the island's shores to be part of the sub-littoral, but in fact is more akin to the edges of the continental shelf, much further offshore.

Hard Ground

Bedrock and areas of boulders (boulder fields), reefs and pinnacles – all hard ground as fishermen call it – once again offers a rich selection of plants and animals. For example, rocky substrate just north-west of the Giant's Causeway supports pink encrusting algae, often seen just underwater on the sides of caves along this coast, various anemones and sea cucumbers. Many more animals thrive in such areas, including starfish of differing sizes and shapes, the stars having from five to fourteen points, one at the end of each 'arm'; colourful sea slugs glide over the rock surfaces, and many fish cluster and lurk around and within reefs and the remains of shipwrecks, common species being ballan wrasse (murrans locally) and other colourful members of this family, coalfish (glashan), pollack (lythe) – the latter two relatives of the cod – and in holes and crevices lurk large conger eels.

The main areas of hard ground are the extension of rocky shore platforms between Portstewart and Portrush, out to depths of around 10 metres, and from about 20 to 25 metres elsewhere along the coastal fringe. These appear to be mainly of basalt types, but off Dunluce the structure indicates that it is white limestone (chalk). There remain uncertainties about the extent of each type.

Grey seal showdown.

Common hermit crab, Pagurus bernhardus.

Rocky and stony reefs are quite plentiful further out amongst sediments such as sand and gravel, including Curran, Scarbh and Solan reefs off the Skerries Islands, the nearby pinnacle of the Storks, a complex of reefs off Benbane Head and the remarkable Shamrock Pinnacle north-west of Rathlin Island, situated in an area noted for sharp snags as the fishermen know them. Many of these reefs and pinnacles are scoured by sand swept along by strong tidal current and exposed to considerable wave action. The Shamrock Pinnacle down to 50 metres (it goes much deeper) was surveyed by divers in 1984 and more extensively in 2009. Due to the strong tidal streams, the area was found to be colonised only by the hardiest of species, such as cluster anemones, sponges and soft corals, notably the puffy white dead man's fingers. These isolated reefs and pinnacles also support brown and red algae where enough light penetrates to them, and they attract shellfish such as lobster and brown crabs, so it is not surprising that they've been known to fishermen for many years.

Sea caves that are partly or fully submerged are also important features along this coast, difficult to survey due to turbulence from tides and waves, although anemones and sponges of conservation interest have been noted. Some partially submerged caves provide shelter for Atlantic grey seals.

Soft Ground

Large areas of the Causeway Coast seabed comprise a mix of sands and gravels of various types, some lying inshore and a great deal further out. Some are derived from former glacial activity and others carried out to sea by rivers such as the Foyle and the Bann. Mixed in with the gravels are shell remains of mussels and clams and suchlike, as well as harder pebbles and cobbles (larger rounded stones). Off the beautiful Causeway coast beaches are cells of sand and gravel that feed these strands, and these are essential for the continued existence and popularity of some of our most visited seaside places.

The detailed seabed Sonar scanning project (completed in 2008) revealed large, mobile sand waves offshore from the Skerries Islands to Benbane Head, some of the most impressive lying off the Giant's Causeway, extending to about 900 metres in length and rising 20 metres above the sea bed. Sand dunes ashore formed and reformed by wind, but these huge underwater rippled sand waves are continuously built up and broken down by tidal streams. Great pot-holes scoured out of the sand lie at the ends of many of these features, places where fish gather, and predators such as porpoise, dolphins and fishermen home in on such aggregations. Fish driven near the surface by underwater predators are caught by diving and plunging seabirds such as guillemots, razorbills, gulls and gannets.

Areas of sand, shell and gravel, swept and disturbed by tides and waves, provide a less secure home for seabed plants and animals than immobile rock. In one sheltered area inside the Skerries is a rare bed of sea grass, and various species of crabs wander over these sediments and burrowing crabs live within the top few centimetres, as do sand eels, an important food item for many diving seabirds, although further surveys are needed to establish the overall biological importance of these large areas of sediments. They can be valuable nursery areas for commercially important fish species such as plaice and bass. Where pebbles and cobbles are mixed with these softer substrates, more diverse communities of algae and animals exist.

The Open Sea

So far this chapter has been about the sea bed, yet there is a considerable variety of life in the water column above Davy Jones's locker (an old expression for the bottom of the sea) to the surface. Life dependent on the open seas and oceans, including marine mammals and seabirds, is usually referred to as pelagic (from the Greek *pelagos*, meaning sea, or it can also mean wanderer when referring to the plankton). Large, sometimes enormous, ocean-going fishing vessels sweep the ocean waters for pelagic fish such as mackerel, herring, sardines and others. Humans are not the only significant hunter-gatherers of the oceans – many of the whales and the basking shark sweep and filter small food items, mostly plankton, from the waters, while toothed whales, dolphins and porpoises pursue and consume fish, crustaceans and squid.

The mixing of Atlantic and North Channel waters off the Causeway Coast, sweeping past islands such as Rathlin and the Skerries, result in turbulence which concentrates small food items, and these attract larger fish which are sought by cetaceans (whales and dolphins) and seabirds. The aggregations above submerged sand waves have already been mentioned, but in the past couple of decades a rising interest in whale-watching, much of this encouraged by the Irish Whale and Dolphin Group, has led to the sighting of species off the Causeway Coast such as minke whales, pilot whales and in 2010 an exceptional sighting of a humpback whale off Rathlin. Dolphins seen include common, striped, Risso's, bottle-nosed and Atlantic white-sided and there are porpoises present most months of the year. Strandings of these animals ashore occur from time to time, adding to our knowledge but always a disturbing event to witness.

Seabirds, notably fulmars and gulls, breed on mainland cliffs from slightly inland Binevenagh west of Coleraine to Kinbane Head close to Ballycastle, and here and there are clusters of kittiwakes, guillemots, razorbills but only where there is water below their breeding sites. The largest colonies are on Rathlin Island, home for several months (May to August) to tens of thousands of guillemots, razorbills, kittiwakes and smaller numbers of puffins, fulmars, shags, black guillemots and five species of gulls. As mentioned in an earlier chapter, some of these seabirds and their eggs also provided food for islanders in the past. Smaller colonies occur on the Skerries, Sheep Island off Ballintoy and Carrick-a-Rede, close to the famous swinging rope bridge. These birds pursue fish and other marine life both close to the sea surface and within plunging and diving depths; guillemots and razorbills are able to dive very deep after fish, down to 50 metres and sometimes much further. Some species follow trawlers and other fishing vessels to scavenge discarded fish, offal and bait, notably fulmars, gannets, kittiwakes and some of the larger gulls.

At the base of all this marine diversity in the pelagic zone – and in the oceans and sea in general - are the unimaginable numbers of tiny floating and drifting, and in some cases swimming, plants and animals of the plankton. In early spring, looking into the waters offshore, or diving through them, visibility is partially obscured by planktonic life, some of it containing, for a few weeks only, the youngest stages of commercial species such as lobsters, crabs and various fish. A scoop of seawater sampled in spring though summer will reveal, under a moderately powered microscope, pulsating life in the forms of weird and wonderful creatures, as well as tiny plants, many also beautiful in structure.

'All flesh is grass' is a saying well known to ecologists, and this applies as much to the open sea as to the land, the 'grass' being the tiny plants, or phytoplankton. What most of us see, and many of us eat, are the next levels up the chain, from crustaceans to fish and whales, the latter sadly still on the menu for some humans.

Off the Menu

This section is about the conservation of marine life, with a local emphasis.

Compared to the French, Spanish and Portuguese, to give just three continental examples, we in Ireland are not major seafood consumers, although this may be changing as celebrity television chefs encourage us to eat more fish and shellfish, and to make sure it is sustainably gathered. Many of the lobsters and other valuable species landed in Northern Ireland are currently exported.

Some fishing practices, such as seabed dredges and trawls, are damaging to the marine environment and the life it supports, and sophisticated electronic fish-finding instruments, navigation aids and massive nets fished from powerful and wide-ranging vessels stack the odds against the fish, and other marine animals. However, fishermen have to make a living and are subject to numerous European laws and restrictions, some of these, notably the requirement to discard perfectly edible fish at sea, not making a lot of sense to these eminently practical folk. Managing marine fisheries, especially those targeting mixed species, is a complex task and depends on good and hard-won scientific information.

As knowledge increases about the species found around the Northern Ireland coast and inshore waters, the number of plants and animals listed as Conservation Priority species (NICP) is increasing: a recent report (2011), excluding vertebrates (animals with backbones, such as fish), lists 46 NICP species in 9 main groups from sponges to seas squirts. Particularly important areas for such species off the north coast are around the Skerries Islands near Portrush and the varied marine habitats at Rathlin Island, which extend into depths of over 200 metres.

As this chapter was being written (autumn 2011), a sizeable area of the submarine environment from Portstewart in the west to Dunseverick in the east, and extending well offshore, is a proposed marine Special Area of Conservation (SAC, see Appendix 1). This will be known as the Skerries/Causeway SAC. The scientific basis for this has been the surveys outlined above, plus historical data. A number of recommendations for further work have been made but there appears to be enough information available now for designation to be completed. Rathlin Island is already an SAC, the boundaries extending up to a kilometre offshore.

A period of consultation is necessary before such designations are confirmed, and representatives of the fishing industry have an opportunity to comment, sometimes expressing concern about the apparently rather wide boundaries and the possible exclusion of some fishing practices.

Shipwrecks

The sea bed along this rugged north coast is the last resting place for many ships, and some passengers and crews, going back over 400 years and possibly much further. Divers, historians, maritime archaeologists, now aided by the details revealed by the multi-beam sonar surveys mentioned above, are recording and studying these shipwreck remains, and finding previously unknown ones. Many are broken apart on rocks, some lie in sand, some are partially covered by sediments and most are festooned with colourful marine life such sponges, hydroids, soft corals and are popular amongst divers. Sea anglers home in on certain wrecks, in search of the abundant fish that inhabit their remains, from large pollack to conger eels.

There are remains of ships sunk during the two world wars, including German U-boats responsible for the fate of a number of vessels along the north and east coasts. Details can be found in Wilson (1997) who, in this third edition, says '...tales of shipwrecks have an irresistible lure.' Rathlin Island has at least 60 known shipwrecks under its turbulent waters, their stories told by the late Tommy Cecil, one of the islanders who attended to Richard Branson's record-breaking balloon when it crashed in July 1987 just off the west tip of the island at the end of its trans-Atlantic voyage.

In the stormy autumn of 1588, ships of the defeated Spanish Armada were struggling home the long way around the tip of north Scotland and down the west coast of Ireland. Some that remained well offshore were more fortunate than those closer in; many of the latter were wrecked by exceptional gales along a coast unfamiliar to these sailors who, although daring and skilful, had only basic navigation instruments and no knowledge of these rugged coasts. The remarkable tale of one survivor is outlined below.

To date, one of the most famous wreck sites is that of the Spanish Armada galleass, the *Girona*, whose story is linked to the Giant's Causeway.

Spanish Treasure

The traditional story that a Spanish Armada ship sank near the Giant's Causeway in 1588 was preserved in local place-names: Port na Spaniagh, Spaniard Rock, Spanish Cave and the Spanish Organ. Numerous nineteenth-century guidebooks and other published accounts of the area, as well as tales told by local guides up to the mid-twentieth century, described how the ill-fated ship foundered in a storm under the rock pinnacles known as the Chimneys. Some claimed the ship had fired her cannons at these rocks, mistaking them for castle turrets, but this seems an unlikely act for the crew of a ship within minutes of disaster.

Why, then, with all these local clues, was it almost 400 years before the Belgian salvage diver Robert Stenuit and his team discovered the few remains and rich contents of this ship at Port na Spaniagh and proved it to be the galleass Girona? In *Treasures of the Armada*, his account of the *Girona* find, Stenuit points out that historical records were inaccurate, tempting divers to search further to the west, in the area between the mouth of the River Bush and Dunluce Castle.

In 1967, on a preliminary visit along the cliff path to Port na Spaniagh, Stenuit and a companion read, in a guidebook they had bought at the Giant's Causeway, how the galleass *Girona* was wrecked at a little cove near the Giant's Causeway, still called Port na Spaniagh. Nobody took the local folklore seriously; but after extensive research, Stenuit – amused to find his theory confirmed in a cheap pamphlet – decided to dive in Port na Spaniagh. On June 27 1967, during his first dive in thirty feet of water at the east face of Lacada Point, he saw a white shape. It was a lead ingot.

Arching my back, I heaved it over, and there stamped on the upper face were five Jerusalem crosses. I had found the wreck.

Nearby, during the same dive, he discovered an Armada cannon, cannonballs and other artefacts. Over the summer diving seasons of 1967, 1968 and 1969, Stenuit and his helpers brought out of Port na Spaniagh a fabulous treasure of gold and silver coins, gold chains, personal jewellery and decorations of the ship's officers and crew, including the Knight of Malta cross belonging to Don Fabricio Spinola, the captain of the Girona. These treasures, and other artefacts recovered from the *Girona* and the *Trinidad Valencera* – another Armada shipwreck, discovered by divers of the Derry Sub-aqua Club in 1971 – are preserved in the Ulster Museum at Belfast, where some are on permanent display. The folklore was right, after all.

Today, the towering columns and jagged rocks of Port na Spaniagh are as awe-inspiring – indeed terrifying – as they must have seemed to the 1,300 or so sailors, soldiers and noblemen who struggled and drowned in this bay on the night of 26 October 1588. There were few survivors; accounts list between five and thirteen, whom James McDonnell of Dunluce helped to return to Spain.

The Reluctant Tourist

I believe that you will be astonished at seeing this letter on account of the slight certainty that could have existed as to my being alive ...

Thus begins an extraordinary first-hand account of a survivor of one of the Spanish Armada ships wrecked off Ireland in the autumn storms of 1588. Captain Francisco de Cuellar was transferred from his ship, the *San Pedro,* to another, one of three wrecked at Streedagh Strand in Co Sligo. Surviving great hardships, Captain de Cuellar spent over three months in the northwest of Ireland, eventually making his way on foot to the vicinity of Dunluce Castle, near the Giant's Causeway (unknown at that time).

... at the end of twenty-one days' journey, I got to the place where Alonzo de Leyva ... with many other gentlemen, were lost ...

He was told by locals:

... of the great misfortunes of our people who were drowned at that place, and [they] showed me many jewels and valuables of theirs, which distressed me greatly.

De Cuellar managed to find help, and was shipped to Scotland and from there collected by a ship from Flanders. He was shipwrecked again off Dunkirk, but survived and eventually reached sanctuary in Spanish-controlled Antwerp, from where he wrote his account in a letter to a friend. This was not published until 1885, in Madrid, as part of a work entitled *La Armada Invinciple* by Captain Caesaro Fernandez Duro, a Spanish naval officer. The narrative 'Captain Cuellar's Adventures in Connacht and Ulster, A.D. 1588' is thrilling reading, and is a rare account of northwest Ireland at the time of Queen Elizabeth I's rule in Britain. Perhaps de Cuellar was the first tourist – albeit a reluctant one – at the Giant's Causeway!

CAPTAIN CUELLAR'S

ADVENTURES

IN

CONNACHT & ULSTER

A.D. 1588.

A PICTURE OF THE TIMES, DRAWN FROM CONTEMPORARY SOURCES.

By HUGH ALLINGHAM, M.R.I.A.,

Member of the Royal Society of Antiquaries (Ireland);
Author of "Ballyshannon: its History and Antiquities," &c.

TO WHICH IS ADDED

An Introduction and Complete Translation

OF

CAPTAIN CUELLAR'S

Narrative of the Spanish Armada

AND HIS ADVENTURES IN IRELAND.

By ROBERT CRAWFORD, M.A., M.R.I.A., &c.

With Map and Illustrations.

LONDON: ELLIOT STOCK, 62, PATERNOSTER ROW.
1897.

LOCATION OF WALKS AND GIANT'S CAUSEWAY

Benbane Head

Dunseverick Walk

Continuation of
Causeway Coast Way

Giant's Causeway

Runkerry Walk

Causeway
Walk

Dunseverick
Castle

A2

PORTBALLINTRAE

Continuation of
Causeway Coast Way

Dunluce
Castle

BUSHMILLS

1:50,000 Sheet 5 O.S.(N.I.)

LANDSCAPE AND WILDLIFE
Where to go, What to see

WALKING IS THE BEST WAY TO APPRECIATE THE LANDSCAPE AND ITS WILDLIFE. THERE IS PLENTY OF CHOICE AT THE CAUSEWAY. THIS CHAPTER DESCRIBES THREE WALKS AND A LONGER TOUR OF THE NEARBY COASTLINE, WHICH CAN BE UNDERTAKEN ON FOOT, BY BICYCLE OR CAR. ALL BEGIN FROM THE GIANT'S CAUSEWAY CENTRE CAR PARKS, EXCEPT FOR THE TOUR, WHICH STARTS AT PORTRUSH.

The aim of the walks and the tour is to encourage exploration of landscape and wildlife, recommending stops at various vantage points or sites of interest. The combination of landscape, habitats and wildlife gives the walker a feeling for the ecology of the area – the ways in which the living things relate to their environment. A bit of local history is slipped in, too, for humans have their own ecology. The walks and the tour follow waymarked paths and signposted roads, and are designed to enable you to see features of the landscape, the variety of habitats and their flora and fauna, without leaving the safety of the paths or roads, which also avoids disturbance.

The emphasis below is on spring and summer, the times when the wildflowers are at their best, birds are breeding and most visitors come to see the Causeway. Autumn and winter have their own beauty, and the Causeway in stormy conditions is a sight to remember – although it should be viewed from a cautious distance!

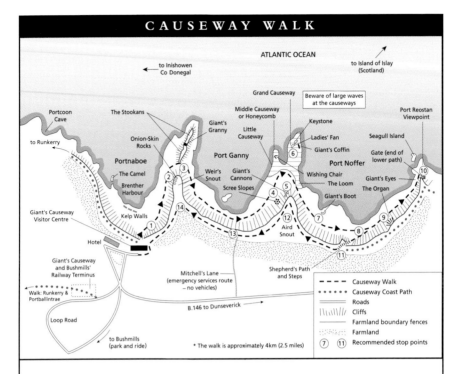

CAUSEWAY WALK

ATLANTIC OCEAN

to Inishowen
Co Donegal

to Island of Islay
(Scotland)

Grand Causeway

Beware of large waves
at the causeways

Portcoon
Cave

The Stookans

Middle Causeway
or Honeycomb

Keystone

Port Reostan
Viewpoint

Giant's
Granny

Little
Causeway

Ladies' Fan

Seagull Island

to Runkerry

Onion-Skin
Rocks

Giant's Coffin

Gate (end of
lower path)

Portnaboe

Port Ganny

6

Port Noffer

The Camel

2

3

Weir's
Snout

Giant's
Cannons

Wishing Chair

Giant's Eyes

10

Brenther
Harbour

Scree Slopes

5

The Loom

The Organ

Giant's Boot

Giant's Causeway
Visitor Centre

14

Kelp Walls

4

1

12

7

9

Hotel

13

Aird
Snout

8

11

Giant's Causeway
and Bushmills'
Railway Terminus

Mitchell's Lane
(emergency services route
– no vehicles)

Shepherd's Path
and Steps

Walk: Runkerry &
Portballintrae

- - - - Causeway Walk

• • • • • Causeway Coast Path

B.146 to Dunseverick

Roads

Loop Road

Cliffs

Farmland boundary fences

Farmland

to Bushmills
(park and ride)

* The walk is approximately 4km (2.5 miles)

7   11 Recommended stop points

Start: At the seaward side of the Visitor Centre.

Finish: Same place (this is a circular walk).

Distance: About 4 kilometres (2.5 miles).

Time: Allow 1.5 to 2 hours, including stops.

Terrain: Surfaced paths, varying from tarmac to stones over soil, uneven in places. Steep stone steps (about 150) linking walk from sea level to cliff-top. Bus available (charge) between Visitor Centre and Causeway, with facilities for wheelchair users (type of transport may vary).

Safety: Steep downhill section at the start of the walk; the Causeway itself is uneven, with some loose rocks. Beware of large waves and unfenced drops at the Causeway. The cliff-top path should be avoided in high winds. The cliff edges can be unstable, so keep to the paths. If the steps are intimidating, you can simply return the way you came, shortening the walk considerably.

Parking: Car parks at the Visitor Centre and Bushmills' park and ride.

Maps: Map 4 or 5 of the Ordnance Survey NI 1:50,000 *Discoverer* series. See sketch map in this chapter for general guidance only.

This walk can be done in either direction, but here it is set out in a clockwise direction, taking you down the hill to the Causeway first. If you prefer to walk down the Shepherd's Steps rather than up, reverse the direction and go along the cliff-top path first (obviously you will have to read this guide differently).

From the **Start**, walk about 100 metres down the hill in front of you to **Stop 1, Portnaboe**. This stop is beside the obvious orange-red exposure of laterite, the crumbly inter-basaltic bed containing iron ore, which is overlaid at the uphill end by glacial deposits of clay and stones. Looking down into the bay on your left (Portnaboe), note the small, spring-fed reed bed near the rocky shore, and the clumps of bramble and bracken amongst the grass and ferns. These are good habitats for birds which spend the spring and summer here, such as grasshopper warblers and whitethroats – rather nondescript and elusive brown warblers – the former with a churring song like the sound of a sewing machine, the latter a more tuneful songster. Sometimes a brown-and-grey hawk, the kestrel, hovers overhead, searching the ground for small prey. Tucked under the cliffs is the Camel Rock, a hard basalt dyke which does look like a camel crouched down; beyond it, fulmars glide to and from their rocky nest sites.

Large eider ducks are often seen bobbing on the sea and resting on the small islands; the males are black and white, and the females are brown. A loud, piping call helps to identify oyster-catchers, black-and-white wading birds which frequent the rocky shore. The low stone walls near the tideline were part of the kelp industry, which died out around the 1930s; seaweed was gathered in winter and spring and spread on these walls to dry, then burned to produce residues rich in useful mineral salts.

The narrow, humped back of the Camel, a hard dyke of rock.

Stop 2. Onion-skin rocks. At the bottom of the hill, on the right, large rounded boulders are set, like currants in a cake, in the purple-red patch of an inter-basaltic bed. These big stones are weathering gradually in layers – hence the name 'onion-skin' rocks. Erosion often loosens them, so keep your distance.

Stop 3. Windy Gap. This is the point where the road continues around the corner, and it is worth a pause; it gives you a wonderful first view (and a photo opportunity) of the Giant's Causeway in the foreground, with

Weathered rocks, known as the 'Onion-skins'.

the towering cliffs and isolated pillars of the Chimneys beyond. On a clear day, the higher parts of the Scottish island of Islay are visible on the horizon. You are now in Port Ganny, the only Causeway bay with a little sand. The steep hills on the seaward side of the gap are the Stookans, so called because their shape resembles that of corn stooks. The thin vegetation and poor soils are easily disturbed, so please avoid the temptation to climb. The pale blue vernal squill – a scarce and beautiful spring plant, closely related to the bluebell, with delicate star-shaped flowers – blooms here in May and June; it is easily seen from the base of the Stookans.

Stop 4. The Little Causeway. The path divides here, a short loop (optional) taking you down past the columns of the Little Causeway and back to the road. The loose stones on the hillside – scree – are typical of the lower slopes of these unstable cliffs. The terrain is inhospitable to plants; nevertheless, in May and June you may see herb Robert (pink, with green or red leaves) and pink-and-white, fleshy-leafed English stonecrop in flower amongst these stones. Look out for ravens – large crows with a deep croak – along the cliffs behind you. The agile, russet Irish stoat is sometimes seen dashing over these screes.

Stop 5. The Giant's Cannons. Poking out of the lower side of the hill are tilted Causeway columns. Vegetation has masked these somewhat. In earlier times they were known as the Giant's Cannons. The slopes above are extremely unstable; do not climb on them.

Stop 6. The Honeycomb (Middle) and Grand Causeways. The Middle and Grand Causeways will thrill you with a memorable impression of how precisely the columns fit together. Note the predominance of five- and six-sided columns. Lichens grow over the Causeway in distinct zones: they are grey near the centre, then vivid yellow, and close to the sea they form a thin black coating, which is often mistaken for oil pollution. Fanciful names – the Wishing Chair, the Keystone, the Giant's Coffin, the Lady's Fan and so on – have been given to some of the arrangements of stones on the Causeways; some are marked on the map for this walk, but a guide is needed to locate most of them. A small buff bird with a white tail is often seen here in summer; this is the wheatear, which manages to raise a brood of young amongst the stones and the numerous visitors before flying south to Africa for the winter. From the Causeway, you can see the Giant's Granny (imagination required!), a bent old lady of stone, on the left-hand side of the Stookans opposite. In spring and summer, the gaps between the Causeway stones are bright with wild flowers such as sea pink, white

A male wheatear – a summer visitor to the rocky Causeway area.

sea campion and more of the pale-blue vernal squill. Offshore, seabirds such as large white gannets pass by, and you might spot an Atlantic grey seal in the water. Looking east across Port Noffer, note the various layers of basalts (lava flows), more reddish soils exposed halfway up, and the remarkable pipe-like columns of the Organ.

Stop 7. The Giant's Boot. This is a large rock about 200 metres past the Causeway, in Port Noffer, sitting where the grass meets the rocky shore. Like the Granny, it is best seen from a particular angle – in this case, from along the path; from this point, it does indeed resemble a huge hiking boot. From its size, it has been calculated that its owner, Finn MacCool, the giant, was sixteen metres (fifty-two feet six inches) tall! This ice- and sea-hewn boulder is marked on maps as the Giant's Chair, but you need to sit on it to realise why! The nearby marshy ground is a fragile habitat for summer-flowering yellow flag iris and spotted orchids, which do not like to be trampled – enjoy them from the Boot or the path.

Stop 8. Port Noffer. The name means 'the Giant's Port'; it is the large bay extending from the Causeway to the headland with the distinctive pinnacles of the Chimneys. Springs and freshwater seepage from the slopes feed this marshy area. In spring and summer, reed buntings, wrens, and sedge and grasshopper warblers call and sing from the reed bed. The dark, wall-like projections of rock on the shore are hard basalt dykes. The shady slopes and cliffs above support woodland-like vegetation, including primroses, violets, wood anemones and woodrush.

A dark band of lichen around the edge of the Giant's Causeway.

Stop 9. The Organ. To reach this, continue along the path in Port Noffer, following it as it rises gradually (at this stage, ignore the sharp right-hand turn halfway up; the walk will bring you back to this). The Organ, which dominates the cliff ahead, is a spectacular group of basalt columns about twelve metres (forty feet) high, with remarkably even cross-fractures giving a building-blocks effect. Grey-green lichen clings to the exposed surfaces. The colonnade changes abruptly to the less regular entablature above. From this viewpoint, enjoy the east prospect of the Giant's Causeway, with the Stookans in the middle distance. The Inishowen peninsula of Co Donegal, running north into the Atlantic, is visible in good weather. You can choose to turn back here and head towards the steps to the cliff-top (see below), or you can continue about 500 metres to the next stop, which is as far as this part of the path goes.

Stop 10. Port Reostan viewpoint. The cliff face next to the path consists of red, purple and grey forms of laterite. The oval hollows in this are made by weathered rocks falling out, leaving sockets known as the Giant's Eyes. A few retain their cores of crumbling basalt. The closure at the end of this path took place in 1994, following severe collapses of the cliff-faces beyond. You can see the remains of a path beyond the gate, but it is very unsafe, so do *not* go any further. This is where you must retrace your steps to the turn in the path mentioned above; by taking the left-hand fork, you will reach the Shepherd's Steps to the cliff-top.

Stop 11. Shepherd's Path and Steps (150+). This path between cliff-top and sea was once used by shepherds and seaweed-gatherers. Halfway up, pause to rest, for the climb is steep. In spring, this is a chance to enjoy the profusion of primroses, violets and early purple orchids on the steep grassy hillside. Later, in summer, the cream flowers of meadowsweet and angelica are buzzing with insects. At the top, the farmed landscape inland is home to fewer wildflowers; but in winter, the barley stubble and damp grassy fields support flocks of whooper swans and geese. Much smaller birds may be sharing these fields: flocks of buff and white snow buntings, twittering brown linnets, and twites, which are similar to linnets but can be distinguished by their twanging call. The birdwatcher's jargon for such easily confused species is 'LBJs' – 'Little Brown Jobs'.

Stop 12. Aird Snout. At the cliff-top, a right turn begins your walk back to the Visitor Centre. The next headland is Aird Snout, which overlooks the Causeway. The black-lichen zone is particularly obvious from here. The small patch of dry heath behind the snout is a rare habitat, purple with heaths and heather in summer, dotted with the pink-and-white flowers of cat's-paw, an uncommon species. From March to June, the gorse along the path in this area is vivid with yellow flowers.

Stop 14. Mitchell's Lane. The fields on either side of this farm lane (the only one along this section of the path) are part of the National Trust's farming and conservation work. Heathland regeneration is encouraged by limiting fertiliser use and controlling grazing. Rabbits help to keep the sward close-cropped, and they share the shelter of the gorse clumps with sheep and small birds such as wrens (tiny and brown, with a loud, rattling song) and black-headed, russet-breasted stonechats (named after their call, which sounds like two pebbles being chipped together).

Stop 15. Weir's Snout. Another narrow headland, and the next good viewpoint. Salty winds and winter grazing keep the grass in the field beside the headland at just the right length to produce a rich growth of wildflowers, including pale-pink meadow thistles, in spring and summer.

The stonechat, a resident bird of the Causeway Coast.

If you complete this walk and are lucky with the weather, the views and the wildlife, you will have had a good introduction to the Giant's Causeway and its natural history. If you just wander along, head down and perhaps chatting to friends, it still should be an enjoyable experience.

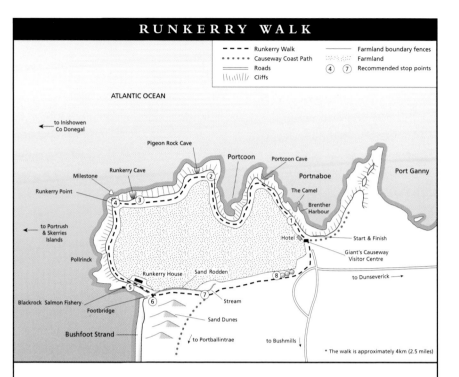

RUNKERRY WALK

- - - - Runkerry Walk	——— Farmland boundary fences
• • • • • Causeway Coast Path	Farmland
===== Roads	④ ⑦ Recommended stop points
⑴⟨⟨⟨/// Cliffs	

ATLANTIC OCEAN

to Inishowen
Co Donegal

Pigeon Rock Cave

Portcoon   Portcoon Cave

Runkerry Cave   Portnaboe   Port Ganny
Milestone   ②   The Camel
Runkerry Point   Brenther
          Harbour
   ④ ③   ①
to Portrush
& Skerries   Hotel   Start & Finish
Islands
              Giant's Causeway
Pollrinck   Visitor Centre

   Runkerry House   Sand Rodden   ⑧   to Dunseverick ➝
Blackrock Salmon Fishery   ⑤
Footbridge   ⑥   ⑦   Stream

Bushfoot Strand   Sand Dunes

       ➚ to Portballintrae   to Bushmills

* The walk is approximately 4km (2.5 miles)

Start: At the seaward side of the Visitor Centre. Turn left; the walk begins along the cliff.

Finish: In the same place (another circular walk).

Distance: 4 kilometres (2.5 miles).

Time: Allow 1.5 hours, including stops.

Terrain: Begins and ends on surfaced paths, but much of the cliff-top section is grassy and slippery when wet. There are some steps, at least two gates and a footbridge over a small stream.

Safety: The cliff-top walk is not recommended in very strong winds. From the sand rodden back towards the Visitor Centre, a small railway train may sometimes be in operation alongside the path. The caves are inaccessible except by boat. Beware of large waves.

Parking: At the Visitor Centre.

Maps: Map 4 or Map 5 of the Ordnance Survey NI *Discoverer* 1:50,000 series. See sketch map in this chapter for general guidance only.

Stop 1. Portnaboe. Follow the cliff-top path past the rear of the Causeway hotel; Stop 1, above Portnaboe, is about 200 metres along, where you have a good view down into the bay on your right. The name means 'Port of the Cow', perhaps because this bay was once grazed by stock. The small harbour used to be a popular location for boat trips to see the caves and the Causeway, but this tradition died out in the 1940s. The leaning, humped rock just beyond the Brenther harbour is a dyke, where lava forced its way up from deep in the Earth through a crack; because of its shape, it is called the Camel. Portcoon Cave, the first of three, lies a little to the west, at a break in the rock platforms, but access is by a side entrance further along this walk. Ravens and kestrels are sometimes seen along this section, and there are good views of the noisy grey-and-white fulmars which occupy the cliffs.

The fulmar, a noticeable cliff-dwelling bird.

Plants of the shoreline include the sweet-smelling, white-flowered scurvy grass; its fleshy leaves are rich in Vitamin C, which prevents scurvy, an unpleasant condition affecting anyone deprived of this vitamin. Long ago, the plant was collected by sailors, who ran short of fresh fruit and vegetables on long voyages.

Stop 2. Portcoon. The name means 'the narrow port or inlet'. A tall rock stack dominates the mouth of this mini-fiord. At Portcoon Cave, visited in the past by local boatmen and their cargo of tourists, the sound of the swell rumbling boulders deep inside and the view back through the Gothic-arched entrance added to the atmosphere of this little-known part of the Causeway.

Stop 3. Runkerry Cave. To see the cave entrance, you need to approach – with care – the grassy edge on the Causeway side. The green and pink algae coating the sea-washed cave walls, and the shiny green fronds of hart's-tongue fern above, give colour to this otherwise sombre cave entrance. Rock doves (ancestors of the common pigeon) and shags (also known as green cormorants) nest inside, and flocks of starlings whir in at dusk to a safe roost. Like all three caves, Runkerry narrows gradually as it runs deep into this headland. Along the base of these cliffs run wave-cut rock platforms, where eiders sometimes sit and a few herring gulls nest, with noisy fulmars cackling from cliffs above.

Stop 4. _Runkerry Point._ A good viewpoint, looking west to the Skerries islands, Portrush and Co Donegal. The name 'Runkerry' has been interpreted as 'the promontory of the pillar stones'. The projecting lump of rock just off this headland, often occupied by shags, is a well-known fisherman's sea marker known as the Milestone. On the headland, look for the horizontal cracks typical of a dyke. The cinder-like gravel and bare black rock here give an idea of how barren this coastline would have been after the lava flows cooled, and the little green rosettes of buck's-horn plantain (so named because the leaves are serrated like a stag's horn) cling tenaciously to this harsh habitat. Black guillemots live around these cliffs – plump, sooty birds with a white flash on each wing. Their thin, reedy calls can sometimes be heard, and if you look at them on the water you may notice their vermilion legs and feet.

Stop 5. _Runkerry House._ This imposing house, with its crow-stepped gables, was originally built in 1883 for Lord Macnaghten, whose family is still associated with nearby Bushmills. Lord Macnaghten's daughters lived here for many years; when the family no longer required the house, it became a home for the elderly, then an outdoor training centre. In 1998-99, under new

Runkerry House.

ownership, it was renovated and new sections were added in the same style, to provide luxury private apartments. The building is made of sandstone, which takes on a warm glow in the evening sun. The small slipway and the poles for hanging nets belong to Blackrock Salmon Fishery, which has not operated for several decades or so as part of the River Bush salmon conservation study. Some of the largest waves along this coast roll into the bay, and when the river is high, a brown, peaty stain of fresh water can be seen across the sea's surface.

Stop 6. *Runkerry footbridge.* The little stream tumbling over rocks to the sea attracts birds such as grey wagtails, yellow below and grey on top. The exposed glacial clays and sandbanks on the beach side of the bridge are riddled with small holes, the nesting sites of sand martins, small, brown, swallow-like birds; look out for them between March and September. This corner of Blackrock Strand is often full of flotsam and jetsam from the sea, including tangles of the brown seaweed, or wrack, once used in the kelp industry, as described above.

Stop 7. *The Sand Rodden.* The rodden — a local name for a rough track — runs from the railway to the beach. The current seasonal train service follows the former tram track along which the Causeway tram trundled between 1887 and 1949. In the scrub, willow warblers and whitethroats sing in spring, and at any time you might hear the squeal of a water rail, a secretive, grey-brown water bird, from the depths of the swamp. Wild leeks, red campion, primroses and bluebells are spring treats along the edges of this little stream, in the shade of the trees.

Stop 8. *Sycamore copse.* Woodland is very scarce on the Causeway coast. Rooks take advantage of these few trees to nest, and are noisily engaged in domestic life from March to June. Between here and the Causeway Centre, you cross the Runkerry Road and pass the train terminus.

DUNSEVERICK CASTLE WALK

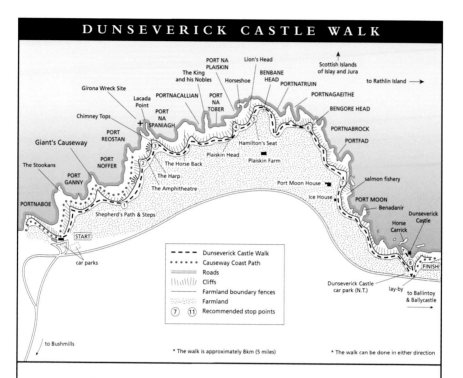

* The walk is approximately 8km (5 miles)   * The walk can be done in either direction

Start: At the seaward side of the Visitor Centre; take the way-marked cliff-top path.

Finish: At Dunseverick Castle; the path meets the B146 road at a lay-by.

Distance: 8 kilometres (5 miles). If you return by road, it is shorter: 4.5 kilometres (2.8 miles).

Time: Allow at least 3 hours, including stops. It is a good plan to have transport parked at Dunseverick Castle, if possible, to bring you back; or check the bus schedule, There is a lay-by and a car park with picnic tables.

Terrain: Surfaced path until a little way beyond the Shepherd's Steps, then grassy for the rest of the walk; in wet weather, it can be very muddy and slippery in places. There are some steps and stiles along the route.

Safety: Not recommended in high winds. Keep well clear of cliff edges, as these are undercut by erosion in many places.

Parking: At the Visitor Centre and Dunseverick Castle. Because the cliffs are high, reaching a maximum of 114 metres (374 feet), binoculars are helpful in spotting some of the features mentioned.

From the **Start**, follow the cliff-top path to the top of the Shepherd's Steps. You can refer to the Causeway walk in reverse (Stops 14 back to 11) for information on this section.

Stop 1 (11 on the Causeway Walk). Shepherd's Steps. Instead of descending the steps, continue east along the cliff-top. On the way to the next stop, you will pass another small area of dry heath, where you may see the stonechat, a bird typical of this coastline. Most of the fenced-off, rough, grazing land extending to the road is owned and managed as a nature conservation area by the National Trust. You may spot some large, russet Irish hares.

Stop 2. The Amphitheatre Bay. From the narrow promontory of Roveran Valley Head, the fine colonnades of the middle basalts are visible on the upper half of the cliffs. The red bed of laterite towards the far point is pitted with Giant's Eyes, almond-shaped cores of partly weathered basalt, most of which are empty sockets where these basalts have fallen out. Numerous fulmars find the columns ideal as nesting sites, and the birds glide about the deep bay on updrafts of air. In spring and summer, the slopes are yellow with kidney vetch and bird's-foot trefoil. The Amphitheatre is prone to major landslides, the scars of which are quite obvious, and what is left of the lower path – now closed permanently – is littered with rock and soil debris.

Stop 3. Chimney Tops. Eighteenth- and nineteenth-century prints show more pillars than now exist; those which remain are isolated from the cliff-face by erosion. Curving into the sea below is Lacada Point, which means 'long flagstone'. It was here the *Girona* foundered on 26 October 1588; when its treasures were recovered in 1967-69, they were mostly found under the stones and boulders of the seabed, at a depth of around ten metres (just over thirty feet), on either side of this point. In Port na Spaniagh Bay, there is a long dyke of dark basalt running into the sea, near which lie the rusting remains of an old navigation buoy (nothing to do with the Armada). The eastern end of this bay shows a purple-blue exposure of the inter-basaltic bed, containing silica, with redder iron ore above.

Stop 4. Plaiskin Head. Leaving Port na Spaniagh, you pass the dipped ridge of The Horseback, the sides of which have many wavy columns. In spring and summer the grassy slopes of these bays are full of wildflowers, including red campion – with many of its colour variations, through pink to white – and look out for clumps of sea pink and the white flowers of sea campion. The cliff-edge vegetation in summer includes creeping willow, the purple devil's-bit scabious and creamy burnet rose. At Plaiskin, there is a chance to see peregrine falcons.

The 'horseshoe' cove below Hamilton's Seat.

Stop 5. Hamilton's Seat. Before arriving at Hamilton's Seat at the west side of Benbane Head notice the horseshoe cove below, and, in the reddish laterite well up the cliff-face, a distinctively shaped projection known as the Lion's Head. At Hamilton's Seat, take time to admire the view back to the west, taking in Plaiskin Head in the foreground and the rugged coastline beyond. The lava flows of the east side of Plaiskin Head are the finest along the whole coast. Natural erosion in the red layer is undermining one of the colonnades of pillars, near the point of the headland. At sea level, the surface of the lower basalts is a crazy-paving of Causeway-like shapes. Buzzards, peregrine falcons and kestrels might put in an appearance while you enjoy this fine landscape.

Stop 6. Bengore Head. The name means 'Peak of the Goats', but it is sheep you may see here, precariously balanced on narrow tracks around the headlands, ever searching for that extra little bit of vegetation to nibble. From Bengore, the cliffs drop in height as they progress eastwards, with the Causeway basalts meeting the white chalk at Portbraddan, by White Park Bay. The view from Bengore towards the Mull of Kintyre in Scotland includes Sheep Island off Ballintoy, Rathlin Island, Fair Head and the island of Sanda off Kintyre, with the cone of Ailsa Craig beyond. Many of the gannets seen offshore nest on this great lump of granite.

Stop 7. Port Moon. The northern grassy promontory of this long bay looks down on Port Fad. From the tip of the point, the entrance to a nineteenth-century bauxite mine can be seen. These old mines are very dangerous and should not be entered. Port Moon has a long history of salmon fishing, and the little red-roofed fishery cottage once looked out on a bag net, set from May through August but now no longer fished. It is said that tea brewed from spring water here will turn milk blue, due to the high copper content of the water. On the stony beaches towards Dunseverick Castle are a few low kelp walls. Across the bay is the jagged profile of Benadanir ('Peak of the Danes'), a favourite perch for peregrine falcons. Buzzards are sometimes seen riding the air currents along the cliffs. As you leave Port Moon, you pass the fishery ice house, long disused, tucked in amidst the gorse on the inland side of the fence-line by the stone steps.

Stop 8. Dunseverick Castle. Fulmars are numerous along the cliffs towards the castle. The Horse Carrick islet below the castle promontory – its shape speaks for itself – may have shags and eiders around it. The ancient fortified promontory of Dunseverick, with the scant remains of the castle, can be reached by steps and a narrow track. Most historians agree that this defensive site has a long history of occupation, possibly going back to pre-Christian times. It was reputedly the end of one of the great early-Christian roads from Tara, and was almost certainly the capital of the Celtic kingdom of Dalriada. Legends claim that St Patrick visited the site. The castle – what remains of it – is more recent. In the sixteenth and seventeenth centuries, it was occupied by a branch of the Ulster O'Cahan family; in the 1640s the O'Cahans lost possession of the castle, and in about 1653 it was destroyed by Cromwellian troops. The ruins visible today were part of the gatehouse. Beyond Dunseverick, to the east, you can see the landscape change to lower headlands and the wide sandy sweep of White Park Bay, backed by slumped chalk cliffs. You have reached the end of the Causeway bays and headlands.

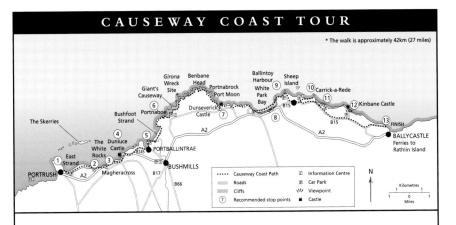

CAUSEWAY COAST TOUR

* The walk is approximately 42km (27 miles)

Girona Wreck Site · Benbane Head · Giant's Causeway · Portnabrock · Portnaboe · Port Moon · Dunseverick Castle · Ballintoy Harbour · White Park Bay · Sheep Island · Carrick-a-Rede · Kinbane Castle · FINISH · BALLYCASTLE Ferries to Rathlin Island · The Skerries · Bushfoot Strand · The Skerries · East Strand · White Rocks · The Dunluce Castle · PORTBALLINTRAE · BUSHMILLS · PORTRUSH · Magheracross

Legend:
• • • • • Causeway Coast Path
══════ Roads
░░░░░ Cliffs
⑦ Recommended stop points
🄸 Information Centre
🄿 Car Park
ᐟᐟᐟ Viewpoint
■ Castle

N

Kilometres
1   0   1
Miles

Start: At the large car park on the east side of Ramore Head, Portrush.

Finish: At Ballycastle sea-front.

Distance: About 32 kilometres (20 miles) by main roads, excluding detours. It is 42 kilometres (27 miles) if walked by the Causeway Coast Path.

Time: At least one day's walk. An energetic day's cycling. An easy run – about half a day – by car.

Terrain: Metalled roads all the way: the A2 from Portrush, diverting to Portballintrae along the B145, back to the A2 through Bushmills, then to the B146 Causeway Road, which rejoins the A2 beyond Dunseverick. Go through Ballintoy on the B15; this will take you along the coast to Ballycastle. There are car parks, lay-bys, picnic sites and toilets reasonably spaced along the route. Cyclists following the recommended route 93 will be diverted along some attractive minor roads. Walkers can follow the way-marked Causeway Coast Way; about two-thirds of this is off-road, following coastal paths.

Maps: Maps 4 and 5 of the Ordnance Survey NI 1:50,000 *Discoverer* series.

In 1989, the Causeway Coast was designated an Area of Outstanding Natural Beauty by the Department of the Environment for Northern Ireland. The AONB, as it is known, extends from Portrush in the west to Ballycastle in the east, along a narrow strip of coastal land covering 4,200 hectares (10,380 acres). It is a diverse landscape of cliff and beach; both coast and hinterland have been occupied by humans for over seven thousand years. The area is quite intensively farmed, and there are few trees except for plantations and shelter-belts around homesteads.

This tour, like the walks, emphasises landscape and natural history. Users with other interests – such as local history, archaeology, architecture, or more detailed geology – will find further information through the Bibliography, and on outdoor panels at some car parks and some viewpoints.

Start: Ramore Head car park, Portrush. Ramore Head, which has been declared an Area of Special Scientific Interest (ASSI) because of its geology, is the culmination of a narrow sill of hard dolerite – an intruded volcanic rock – around which the holiday resort of Portrush has developed. The two sandy beaches, to the west and the east, have contributed to the resort's popularity. The lava forced up from the Earth to create Ramore Head also made the little archipelago of islands offshore, known as the Skerries. Like most of the nearby Causeway headlands, these are tilted, with rugged, stepped cliffs facing the Atlantic breakers, while the spray-splashed land behind slopes gently away from the sea. Along the low, rocky shoreline facing the east strand is the National Nature Reserve, which contains the famous 'Portrush rock', source of eighteenth-century hot debates on the origin of basalt. More information is available at the nearby Portrush Countryside Centre.

The Giant's Head – chalk cliffs near Portrush.

Stop 2: Whiterocks car park. Whiterocks is also a geological ASSI. Walk the short distance down to the beach to view the sea-eroded chalk cliffs. The Giant's Head stands out a little to the east, and close inspection of the chalk outcrops along the Whiterocks end of the beach will show bands of brown flints and occasional bullet-like fossils. These are belemnites, an extinct relative of the squid. The unusual convex shape of the long beach between Portrush and here is due to wave refraction by the Skerries islands, which affects the way the sea sculpts this shoreline. Various methods of erosion control have been tried here, with golfers particularly anxious to protect the championship course behind the mobile dunes. Green-and-red burnet moths and banded snails live amongst the sharp marram grass.

Stop 3: Magheracross car park and viewpoint. It is worth pausing at this excellent vantage point, with its information panels. Looking back towards Portrush, there is another good view of the pillars and arches of the eroded chalk cliffs. In May and June, many salt-tolerant plants brighten the grassy slopes by the road and the cliff ledges: sea pink, red campion, white sea campion, scurvy grass, yellow kidney vetch, purple thyme and, here and there on the cliffs, the shiny green leaves of sea beet. In winter, flocks of curlews feed in the damp fields across the road. Look east towards Dunluce Castle, and note the change to dark basalt, with the Causeway headlands beyond.

Stop 4: Dunluce Castle. A tour of this, the most spectacular north-coast castle, is a pleasant diversion. The promontory has been occupied for about 1,500 years, since the Iron Age, and the first castle was built by the Normans around AD1300. The castle contains the remains of a Jacobean manor house, and the site was home to MacQuillans and McDonnells before it was abandoned in 1660. Recent excavations by archaeologists beside the castle have revealed a paved roadway, remains of stone and wooden homes, jewellery and pottery, all part of the 1608 town of Dunluce. Ravens and peregrine falcons, suitably noble birds, inhabit this famous ruin and its imposing cliffs.

Stop 5: Portballintrae Beach car park. A diversion down the Bayhead Road (B145) to Portballintrae, a short distance from Dunluce Castle, is worthwhile. In the 1930s, the horseshoe crescent of the bay was lined by a broad sandy beach; but sea erosion carried most of the sand away, and by the 1980s there was only a narrow strip remaining. Erosion continues – note the many examples of reinforcement and protection needed to keep the houses safe from collapse,

Atlantic swell at Bushfoot Strand.

and to trap any new sand washed up. As one local resident commented, even his woodworms wear lifejackets! The variety of shore habitats – soil and gravel exposures, rock, seaweed and a little sand – attract a rich variety of birds. In summer, sand martins nest in the eroded sandbanks and white sandwich terns call noisily as they fish in the bay. Winter provides up to ten species of wader: silvery-grey sanderlings, brown ringed plovers, turnstones (mottled brown waders which flip over pebbles and seaweed in search of food), slate-coloured purple sandpipers and others feed and roost between the bay and the mouth of the River Bush, below the car park at the end of the shore road. This is a good place to see surfers in action, as some of the biggest waves on the coast roll in year-round, given unsettled conditions offshore. Occasional porpoises also enjoy the surf.

Stop 6: Giant's Causeway Centre car parks. Motorists have to double back from Stop 5, passing through Bushmills, to reach the Causeway. Walkers and cyclists can cross the footbridge at the mouth of the River Bush and join the railway route to Stop 6. The woodlands surrounding Dundarave Estate outside

Bushmills are private. They are an important refuge for woodland birds on this otherwise rather treeless coast; summer-visiting blackcaps and chiffchaffs lurk here, and one or two pairs of buzzards nest within, cruising on broad wings over the surrounding fields to hunt rabbits. Routes around the Causeway are described above. The Visitor Centre provides a wealth of information on the Causeway Coast, and the shops stock a good range of books, leaflets and other goods.

Stop 7: Dunseverick Castle car park. The car park on the cliff side of the cottage has picnic tables, and more room than the lay-by. The lay-by has a useful information panel on the wall. Dunseverick, like Dunluce, is a stone castle on a strategic cliff-bound promontory. Little of the original castle remains, but, as the panel describes, this site has a long history of occupation and strife. Rock doves and jackdaws often lurk on the castle walls, constantly exposed to the threat of attack by peregrine falcons. In early summer, the wet hollow below the castle is bright with yellow flag irises. The Scottish islands of Islay and Jura – Islay in front, the hills of Jura behind – lie offshore to the north, and Rathlin Island's black-and-white cliffs, once likened to a drowned magpie, can be seen closer to the Antrim coast.

Stop 8: White Park Bay. There are two viewpoints – the car park by the Youth hostel (medium size) and a lay-by just east of this (small). The lay-by has the better view, taking in the sandy sweep of the bay from the top of the chalk cliffs. The lumpy profile of the grasslands is due to slumped blocks of chalk, which sit uneasily on slippery Lias clay. These fossil-rich clay beds are occasionally exposed in streams and on the lower shore. One of the mounds directly below the lay-by, partially ringed with stones, is a Neolithic burial site, a reminder of occupation of the bay about 5,000 years ago. White Park Bay is another ASSI, with its interesting land forms and scarce plants such as adder's tongue, moonwort – said to cause horses to cast a shoe if they step on it – and many species of orchids.

Stop 9: Ballintoy Harbour. The harbour is reached by the twisting and narrow road that passes the white Ballintoy church and the extraordinary architecture of Ben Dhu House, built by an artist; the design of this house has prompted one purist to describe it as a construction 'of staggering eccentricity and inappropriateness'. In the nineteenth century the harbour was used to export limestone products, and the lime kilns at the car park dominate this picturesque place. Faulting has created a moonscape of jumbled and tilted basalt

Disused limekilns at Ballintoy Harbour.

sea stacks, dropping them below the level of the older chalk cliffs. The coves are a haven for eider ducks, oystercatchers and other waders; in spring and summer, wildflowers – blue vernal squill, pale-yellow kidney vetch, mauve rock spurrey and purple thyme – cling to the rock stacks. From the pier, nesting cormorants and other seabirds on Sheep Island can be seen just offshore, with the high cliffs of the west end of Rathlin Island further out. From the white church, you can walk to Larrybane, at the entrance to the next site, along a field and cliff-top path with fine views.

Stop 10: Carrick-a-Rede. Carrick-a-Rede is accessed just east of Ballintoy village, on the curve of the road up Knocksoghey Hill. There is a spectacular cliff-top walk from the car park to Carrick-a-Rede, which is the largest of three islands close to the shore. The nearest island is joined to the mainland by a swinging rope bridge (opening hours vary seasonally), originally erected by salmon fishermen over the fishing season (mid-April to the end of September). The modern, strenghtened bridge is now managed by the National Trust as the fishery closed in 2002. The rope bridge experience has become extremely popular and on very busy days, especially in summer and on bank holidays, there may be a timed ticket system operating. This is to minimise queues to cross the bridge. On reaching the site, not everyone wishes to cross. Common sense dictates that if you are uneasy, don't cross (remember you have to return!). National Trust staff are on site daily, during normal opening hours, to advise visitors on safety.

Dolerite – a hard volcanic rock – and chalk were both mined at Larrybane, dolerite in the nineteenth century and chalk from the 1930s to the 1970s. A huge lime kiln stands beside a small café at the edge of the car park. On the Carrick-a-Rede islands, basalt dominates, with ash layers in the north- and west-facing cliffs. Sixty million years ago, this was an explosive volcano, and today seabirds (razorbills, guillemots, kittiwakes and fulmars) nest amongst the shattered and eroded rocks and ash. The fishery dates from the seventeenth century, and Carrick-a-Rede is generally translated as 'the rock in the road' – the 'road' being the east-to-west sea route of migrating Atlantic salmon.

Stop 11: Portaneevey car park. Portaneevey – 'the Port of the Caves' – lies below these cliffs. The viewpoint at the fenced-off cliff-top, approached by a surfaced path, is worth a visit for the outlook to Carrick-a-Rede and the more distant vista of islands, mountains and cliffs, from Fair Head across to Scotland. The view is well interpreted by information panels.

Stop 12: Kinbane Castle. A narrow road leads to a car park. From here, past the tiny, grassy-roofed ice house (which once served the former salmon fishery in the bay below), a path becomes a long set of steep steps descending to a remote cove. At the base of the beautiful, narrow chalk headland of Kinbane sit the remains of another stone castle, built in 1547 by Colla Dubh McDonnell, elder brother of Sorley Boy McDonnell of Dunluce Castle. The castle was still occupied in the mid-eighteenth century, but now all that remains is a gate tower and some flanking walls. These remains are unstable in places and should be treated with care. Just off the headland, the Atlantic swirls and boils on Carrickmannon – the rock of Manannán, an Irish sea god, a trickster and shape-shifter, whose name is also linked with the Isle of Man in the Irish Sea. The dark basalt outcrop of Gobe Feagh – Ravens' Point – towers over the west end of the small bay, with prostrate clumps of juniper clinging to the terraced soil slips on its slopes.

Stop 13: Ballycastle – North Street viewpoint. As you descend the steep hill approaching Ballycastle's seafront, the beach, Fair Head and Rathlin Island become visible. By now you have left the Causeway Coast Area of Outstanding Natural Beauty and entered the equally beautiful Glens of Antrim. Two ferries run regularly, weather permitting, from the harbour to and from Rathlin Island – summer haunt of tens of thousands of seabirds and home to at least 130 resident islanders, a vibrant and welcoming community.

POSTSCRIPT

With a few exceptions, I have kept myself out of this book. However, almost six decades on from my first field trip to the area, some sort of conclusion and forward vision seems appropriate.

An American journalist whom I took on a tour by the coastal route from the Glens of Antrim to Derry City in 1987 was very impressed by the variety of scenery within, to him, such a short distance. He commented that at home, he would have to drive up, down and across several states to see such a range of landscapes and seascapes. This emphasised to me the need to care for this part of the Antrim and Derry coastal strip and its hilly hinterland.

I live in hope that such care will happen. The pressures on this area are obvious, are increasing and are discussed in this book. The emergence of a new generation of scientists and fieldworkers and the sophisticated technology available to them has greatly increased the knowledge necessary for protection of landscapes and their wildlife and the marine environment. European legislation, National and Regional and Local Government, non-Government organisations, local communities and visitors are all essential ingredients in finding a sustainable balance.

An incident back in 1986 reminds me of all this. A local duck-keeper at a settlement just along the road from the newly opened Giant's Causeway Visitor Centre was concerned that the increase in tour coaches and traffic in general would result in his ducks becoming road casualties. Hens scatter when alarmed but ducks cross a road in an unhurried and orderly manner. He put up a home-made, hand-painted sign, the words compressed, that read 'SLOWDUCKS'. I was unable to decide whether this meant 'go slow, there are ducks' or that the ducks themselves were slow. Clarification came a few months later, when the sign was taken down and a new one erected: 'POWERFUL SLOWDUCKS'. The qualification demonstrated the wry humour of the north Antrim folk, confirmed how slow the ducks were, and suggested that duck mortality had not decreased in the interval.

It is small things like this that matter. Visitors' (and locals') cars today back up behind large tractors and tour coaches, especially in the busy summer months on these narrow roads leading to the Causeway and other popular destinations. Tolerance is needed on all sides. I look forward with a mix of optimism and concern, and hope that the former prevails.

Philip S. Watson

APPENDIX 1
Designations

A number of international, national, regional and local designations of protective and conservation relevance have been declared around the Causeway Coast. The following are the most relevant:

World Heritage Site – Giant's Causeway

The World Heritage Convention seeks to promote international co-operation in the protection of sites which are of exceptional interest and of universal value. In 1986, the Convention added the Giant's Causeway, including seventy-one hectares of adjacent coastline, to its list of sites and monuments. The Causeway meets two of the criteria for an outstanding natural property: it is a prime example of the Earth's evolutionary history during the Tertiary epoch; and it contains rare and superlative natural phenomena. The outstanding cultural value of the nearby wreck of the *Girona* is also recognised, as it is a nautical archaeological site associated with an event of international historical significance.

National Nature Reserve – Giant's Causeway

In 1987, the Giant's Causeway, with seventy-one hectares of adjacent coastline, was designated a National Nature Reserve by the Department of the Environment for Northern Ireland. National Nature Reserves are managed specifically to conserve nature and to promote education and research. The Department works closely with the National Trust, which owns and manages the reserve, to ensure that the site is protected and that visitors are given the opportunity to discover and enjoy the geological wonders and wildlife of the Causeway and the surrounding cliffs. Another National Nature Reserve on the Causeway Coast is the Portrush Sill.

Causeway Coast Area of Outstanding Natural Beauty

The north coast of Co Antrim, between Portrush and Ballycastle, including the Giant's Causeway, is one of the most spectacular coastlines in Europe. The Department of the Environment for Northern Ireland designated the Causeway Coast Area of Outstanding Natural Beauty in 1989. This designation formally recognises that the coast and adjacent farmland is a landscape of national importance. The purpose of this designation is to help protect – and, where possible, improve – this landscape, for the benefit of those living in the area and of the many visitors who come to see and enjoy its natural beauty. The Antrim Coast and Glens Area of Outstanding Natural Beauty (including Rathlin Island) is adjacent to the Causeway Coast; it begins just west of Ballycastle town.

Areas of Special Scientific Interest

These are areas deemed to be of scientific interest by reason of their wildlife, their natural vegetation, or their geological, physiographical or other special features. The Department of the Environment for Northern Ireland has designated a number of such areas on the Causeway Coast – for example, Ramore Head and Skerries, Portballintrae, Runkerry, White Park Bay, Sheep Island and Carrick-a-Rede.

Special Area of Conservation (SAC)

These are areas given protection under the European legislation of the Habitats Directive. They are designated because of possible threats to habitats or species which they contain and to provide protection to a variety of plants, animals and habitats of importance to biodiversity both on a national and international scale. Parts of the mainland of the Causeway Coast are included in the North Antrim coast SAC, and the whole of Rathlin Island and an area of sea around it are an SAC.

Special Protection Area (SPA)

These are designated under the European Commission Directive on the Conservation of Wild Birds (The Birds Directive). They are internationally important areas for breeding, over-wintering and migrating birds. Sheep Island and Rathlin Island are the two relevant north coast SPAs.

Marine Conservation Zone (MCZ)

An area of sea around Rathlin Island comprising 90.57 square kilometres was awarded this designation in 2017. The purpose is to protect an unusually deep sea bed, the small population of black guillemots and sub-tidal geological and geomorphological features.

Many organisations, from government departments to local organisations, have roles on the Causeway Coast. The following is a summary of key contacts. Tourist Information Centres and local authority offices can provide further information, and check out websites and contacts listed in the bibliography

How to find the Giant's Causeway.

The Giant's Causeway is situated on the north coast of County Antrim, 3 km north of the town of Bushmills. The Causeway's Irish grid reference is C946447. Relevant maps are the Ordnance Survey of Northern Ireland 1:50,000 scale sheets 4 (Coleraine) and 5 (Ballycastle) of the *Discoverer* series.

Access is from the B146 road, off the A2. Cyclists can follow the National Cycle Network Route 93. For public transport contact Translink, the main organisation responsible for train and bus services throughout Northern Ireland. There is a park-and-ride service between Bushmills and the Giant's Causeway Visitor Centre, and a shuttle service between this centre and the Giant's Causeway. The nearest train stations are at Portrush and Coleraine, and a small heritage railway operated seasonally between Bushmills and a loop road close to the Causeway Visitor Centre.

Visitor Information Centres are located in Portrush, the Giant's Causeway Visitor Centre, Bushmills (seasonal) and Ballycastle.

The *Local Authority* for the area is the Causeway Coast and Glens Borough Council, based in Ballycastle. Contact www.causewaycoastandglens.gov.uk

National Trust – staff are present in the Visitor Centre. General information is available on nt.org.uk/days-out/northern-ireland

Causeway Coast and Glens Heritage Trust – based in the village of Armoy, south of Ballycastle. Contact www.ccght.org

Coastguard – dial 999 and ask for the Coastguard

Other useful websites:

Rathlin Island community website – www.rathlincommunity.org
Royal Society for the Protection of Birds – www.rspb.org/northernireland
Local and regional transport – www.translink.co.uk
Tourism - Northern Ireland Tourist Board – www.nitb.com

ACKNOWLEDGEMENTS

Many people, including staff of numerous organisations, have helped with information, and in other ways, over the twenty years since the first version of this book was published in 1992.

The author thanks the following individuals: Robert Anderson, Linda May Ballard, Ruth Blair, Joe Breen, Gary Burrows, Tommy Cecil, Cahal Dallat, Phil Davidson, Hill Dick, Roger Dixon, Philip Doughty, Sammy Gault, Claire Goodwin, John E. Greer, Mike Hartwell, Gary Hewitt, Frank Holden, David and Robert Hutchinson, Ian Irvine, Johnny Johnston, James Kane, George and Evelyn Kane, Morris McCurdy, Andrew McDowell, Tom McDonald, Tom McDonnell, Liam and Alison McFaul, Neil McFaul, Peggy McFaul, Kevin McGarry, Bertie McKay, Brona Moffett, Ross Millar, Sean Morton, Robin Ruddock, David Speers and Ian Wilson.

The Northern Ireland Environment Agency provided reports and other information which greatly helped in the writing of several chapters, as did the National Trust, the Royal Society for the Protection of Birds and the Department of Agriculture, Environment and Rural Development. The National Museums of Northern Ireland, notably the Ulster Museum and the Ulster Folk and Transport Museum, were also helpful in sourcing information, as were the North-East Education Board's libraries. Thanks are also due to the Northern Ireland Tourist Board, the Public Record Office of Northern Ireland, the University of Ulster at Coleraine, the Causeway Coast and Glens Heritage Trust and the Bushmills Folklore and History Group.

From the first O'Brien Press edition in 2000 to this new and enlarged version, my original manuscripts have been greatly improved by my editor Susan Houlden and I am most grateful for her patient guidance, and to all others who helped at O'Brien Press in Dublin.

Finally, the patience and support of my wife Kay, and the support and skills of my two children (John Stewart Watson, publisher and Kari Owers, Public Relations) made possible this publication and the many years of research and field work behind it – my heartfelt thanks to all three.

PICTURE CREDITS

The author and publisher thank the following for permission to use photographs and illustrative material: National Museums Northern Ireland, colour section 1, pp.6 and 7 (top) 'East Prospect of the Giant's Causeway (1739)' by Susanna Drury (1733–1770); Welch print, 'Naturalists at the Causeway 1868', pp.26 and 27, Welch print, 'In the Wishing Chair, Giant's Causeway', p.44, Welch print 244, 'Giant's Well', p.49; W.A. Green Collection 263, 'Kelp Burning', p.36; photographer Bernard Picton, p.71, colour section 1, p.8 (top); colour section 2, *Girona* treasure, p.8 (top); photographer Claire Goodwin, p.74, colour section 1, p.8 (bottom), colour section 2, p.8 (bottom); National Trust, pp.13, 16, 63, 65, colour section 1, p.2 (top), p.5 (bottom); Northern Ireland Environment Agency, pp. 1, 19, 23, 28, 29, 82, 86, 87, 88, 90, 97, 102, 104, colour section 1, p.1, p.2 (bottom), p.3 (both), p.4 (both), p.5 (top), p.7 (bottom); colour section 2, p.1 (bottom), p.2 (bottom), p.3 (top), p.4 (top), p.6 (both) p.7; J. Taylor, p.10, colour section 2, p.5; D. Speers, p.33; the late Miss Peg Pollock, p.38 (both), p.45; Tom McDonald, p.34 (top); Tom McDonnell, author photo p.3, p.73, colour section 2 p.1 (top), p.3 (bottom), p.4 (bottom); Robert

Anderson, p.37; Author's own pictures, pp.14, 18, 40, 68, 85, 92, 93, 102, colour section 2, p.2 (top), p.6 (top); Author's collection, pp.11, 12, 20, 37, 41, 46, 51, 52, 56, 57, 100; colour section 2, p.5 National Trust, photographer Roger Kinkead. Front cover photograph: iStockphoto. Back cover photograph: Shutterstock.

BIBLIOGRAPHY

Numerous sources were used as references in the writing of this book. The following is a selection of key references and recommended further reading. Useful local sources include *The Bann Disc* (Journal of the Coleraine Historical Society), *The Glynns* (Journal of the Glens of Antrim Historical Society* and *Portcaman* (Journal of the Bushmills Folklore and History Group.

Anglesea, M. and J. Preston., 1980. *A Philosophical Landscape: Susanna Drury and the Giant's Causeway*. Art History, 3, pp. 252-273.

Brett, C.E.B. and M. O'Connell, 1996. *Buildings of County Antrim*. Ulster Architectural Heritage Society and the Ulster Historical Foundation, Belfast.

Cecil, T. 1990. *The Harsh Winds of Rathlin: Stories of Rathlin's Shipwrecks*. Impact Printing, Coleraine.

Dallat, C., 1990. *A Tour of the Causeway Coast*. Friar's Bush Press, Belfast.

Dallatt, C., 1990. *Antrim Coast and Glens: A Personal View.* HMSO, Belfast.

Dawson, N., 1996. 'The Giant's Causeway Case: Property Law in Ireland 1845-1995'. In, *One Hundred and Fifty Years of Irish Law*, N. Dawson, D. Greer and P. Ingram (Eds.), The Queen's University of Belfast.

Erwin, D. and B. Picton. 1987. *Guide to Inshore Marine Life*. The Marine Conservation Society, Immel Publishing, London.

Faulkner, J. and R. Thompson. 2011. *The Natural History of Ulster*. National Museums Northern Ireland.

Gallagher, L. and D. Rogers, 1992. *Castle, Coast and Cottage: The National Trust in Northern Ireland*. The Blackstaff Press (second edition), Belfast.

Groves, A., 2016. *A souvenir guide Giant's Causeway County Antrim*. The National Trust.

Hall, S., 2010. *The Giant's Causeway*, retold by Daniel Ferguson, designed and illustrated by Stephen Hall. Earth Native Art (Fifth Edition).

Hammond, F., 1991. *Industrial Heritage – Antrim Coast and Glens*. HMSO, Belfast.

Kane-Smith, G., 2011. *Georgie's Causeway: a peopled history of the Giant's Causeway.*

Published by the author, printed by W and G Baird Ltd., Belfast.

Kennedy, A. 2008. 'In search of the "true prospect": making and knowing the Giant's Causeway as a field site in the seventeenth century'. *British Journal for the History of Science* 41 (1): 19-41, March 2008.

Lyle, P, 2010. *Between Rocks and Hard Places: Discovering Ireland's Northern Landscapes.* Geological Survey of Northern Ireland, Department of Enterprise, Trade and Investment, Belfast.

Lyle, P., 1996. *A Geological Excursion Guide to the Causeway Coast.* Department of the Environment, Northern Ireland.

Marshall, J., 1991. *Forgotten Places of the North Coast.* Clegnagh Publishing, Mosside, County Antrim.

National Trust, 2007. *Shifting Shores: Living with a changing coastline.* The National Trust, Northern Ireland.

Somers, D., 2005. 'Naked Among the Savages - The Adventures of Captain Franscisco de Cuéllar 1588-9', in, *Endurance: Heroic Journeys in Ireland*, pp. 55-80. The O'Brien Press, Dublin.

Tilley, C. and Cameron-Daum, K. 2017. *An Anthropology of Landscape.* UCL Press, London.

Watson, P.S., 2011. *Rathlin: Nature and Folklore.* Stone Country Press, Glasgow.

Wilson, I., 1997. *Shipwrecks of the Ulster Coast.* Impact Printing Ltd. (third edition), Coleraine.

The following are websites of relevant organisations providing further scientific and technical information and publications. Marine and submarine data and reports can be sourced through the NIEA, NMNI and Seasearch websites.

www.bgs.ac.uk/gsni (Geological Survey Northern Ireland)

www.habitas.org.uk (Ulster Museum-based scientific and literature resource)

www.marine.ie/home/services/surveys/seabed/JIBS.htm (Joint Irish Bathymetric Survey)

www.ni-environment.gov.uk (Northern Ireland Environment Agency)

www.nmni.com (National Museums of Northern Ireland)

www.science.ulster.ac.uk/esri/Centre-for-Maritime-Archaeology (Centre for Maritime Archaeology, based at the Coleraine campus)

www.seasearch.co.uk/northernireland (Seasearch)